Swan Street in about 1920 with the Bell Inn, Spurgeons Stores (then the Post Office) and the Almshouses.

ISBN 0 9513106 0 7

Published by Halstead and District Local History Society.

Printed by Colne Valley Printers Limited, 12 Head Street, Halstead, Essex.

Further copies are available from the author at The Maltings, North End Road, Little Yeldham, Halstead, Essex. CO9 4LE.

Price £3.50.plus 50p postage and packing.

AUTHOR'S PREFACE AND ACKNOWLEDGEMENTS

"A Pictorial History of Sible Hedingham" was collated and written by me at the request of Roy Tanner, the Chairman of Sible Hedingham Parish Council. It was considered that much had been previously written about the history of Sible Hedingham but never a book containing photographs of the village. It was feared that unless a book was published, many old photographs and the information about them would be lost forever. I was therefore commissioned by Roy Tanner to collect old photographs of the village and select the most interesting for inclusion in this book with suitable and informative captions. In this, I have endeavoured to include, not only street scenes and the principal buildings, but also the residents at work and recreation, the industries and crafts and in particular to record something of the contribution made by the village and its residents in the two World Wars. Principally, the illustrations are prior to 1950 and comprise only part of the total collected. I would like to express my grateful thanks to Roy Tanner and the members of Sible Hedingham Parish Council for inviting me to compile this book which has given me the greatest pleasure.

I have always taken a keen interest in the history of Sible Hedingham and some of the photographs in this book were collected by me many years ago. It is sad to recall that some of the donors have since passed away including:–

Percy Ralph Bareham
Harry Broyd
Fred and Sarah Corder
May Corder
Walter and Ethel Corder
William Corder
Albert Redgewell
Lily Rippingale (Gestingthorpe)
Len Smith (Castle Hedingham)
Stanley and Bessie Springett
Edgar (Ned) and Alfred (Arkie) Spurgeon

Apart from my own family (the Corder family) it was perhaps the late Ned and Arkie Spurgeon who did much to encourage my interest in the history of Sible Hedingham and much of the information and several of the photographs came from them.

More recently numerous other people have assisted me with the loan of photographs, information and proof reading including:–

Sid and Doris Allen
Percy Bamberger
Janet Barber
Wilfred and Beatrice Birch
Charles Bird
Cecil Boorer

Cleone Branwhite
Jack and Joy Brett
Bess Burder
Percy and Edith Corder
Florence Cowlin
Eve Faulkner
Victor Gray, M.A., (County Archivist)
May Halls
Robin Harding
Audrey and Robert Hardy
Ian Harrington
Lily Harrington
Rodney Hatfield
Frank and Violet Headland
Henrietta A.V. Lodge
Alec Metson
Frederick W. Pawsey, D.F.C., J.P.
Julia Payne
John Redgewell
Frances Ripper
Norman and Phyllis Ripper
Winifred Ripper
Rev. Barry Rodwell (former Rector of Sible Hedingham)
Alfred and Iris Ruffle
Arthur Ruffle
Richard Shackle (Colchester Library)
Kenneth Stanhope, F.Inst.L.Ex.
Roy Tanner
Errol Lincoln Uys
Jean Whiting
Ted and Chris Wilson (The Museum of the Working Horse, Toppesfield)
Archie and Violet Wright

I would like to express my grateful thanks to all the above and in particular to Jean Whiting who collected many of the photographs used in this book and to Lily Harrington who lent photographs and provided much valuable information.

Some illustrations and information have been obtained from the Essex Record Office, Colchester Central Library, Chelmsford Library and the archives of the Halstead and District Local History Society. The archivists, librarians and staff have been most helpful and I have been much encouraged by them and by the committee of the Halstead and District Local History Society.

It was of enormous benefit in the compilation of this book, to have access to the back issues of the Halstead Gazette and I would like to record special thanks in this respect to Liz Tolfts, Dave Osborne and Geoffrey Root. The old copies of the Gazette provided the basis for the record of Sible Hedingham men who served in the First World War, in particular, but additional information was forthcoming from the following:–

The museum of the Northamptonshire Regiment
The Royal Garrison Artillery Library
and The Essex Regiment Museum whose Curator, David Jones and assistants Peter Redman and Brain Clayton have been most helpful.

The photographs have been carefully copied by John Abbott, Harry Cole and Arthur Morgan and the book printed by Colne Valley Printers Limited to whom I am most grateful.

The Foreword was written by Roy Tanner who also launched the book. He has been a tremendous support in many respects and I greatly appreciate his assistance and interest.

Finally I trust this book will give enjoyment to all its readers and to some, bring back happy memories of this large and interesting North Essex village.

Adrian Corder-Birch, F.Inst.L.Ex., M.I.C.M.,
The Maltings, North End Road,
Little Yeldham, Halstead, Essex.

April 1988

FOREWORD

by

ROY TANNER

Chairman of the Sible Hedingham Parish Council

The Parish Council felt it was important to try and collect photographs and stories of Sible Hedingham in days past, to show present and future generations.

Adrian Corder-Birch was asked to research and if possible to write this book. We could not have found a better author as he has strong family ties with Sible Hedingham and his special relationship with the Spurgeon Brothers meant he had a wealth of memories and photographs to commence with.

Sible Hedingham with its long industrial history of Farming, Maltings, Brickyards and Wood Joinery is a village to be proud of and I hope you enjoy reading this book and learn something new about Sible Hedingham's past.

G.R. Tanner
Washlands Farm,
Sible Hedingham,
Halstead, Essex.

April 1988

CONTENTS

Introduction
Map
St. Peters Church
The Church Choir, Bell Ringers and a Burial
Sir John Hawkwood
The Rectory
The Friendly Societies Parades to the Church
The Baptist Church
Schools
The Almshouses
Street Scenes
Some principal houses
Village shops
Public Houses, Hotels, Inns and Taverns
The Cut Maple and Tower Windmills
Alderford and Hulls Watermills
The River Colne
Some village crafts, occupations and industries
The Brick, Tile, Pottery and Drain Pipe making industry
Hedingham bricks in use
The Castle and Sible Hedingham Joint Fire Brigade
A fire at Rippers woodworks
The development of Rippers Limited
The Colne Valley and Halstead Railway through Hedingham
More Public Transport and Haulage
The First and Second World Wars
The Sible Hedingham Brass Band and Dance Bands
The Plaza Cinema
Football, Bowls, Cricket and Tennis
Sible Hedingham Scouts
One final scene

INTRODUCTION

The village of Sible Hedingham in terms of area is the second largest in Essex covering an area of over five thousand acres. It is situated in the north of the county and on the west bank of the River Colne. On the east bank, opposite, is the historic but smaller village of Castle Hedingham with its splendid Norman Keep.

It is thought that the name 'Hedingham' is derived from the 'ham of Hedin's people' and 'Sible' from the family of Sibil, widow of Geoffrey de Laventon, who held land in Sible Hedingham in 1237.

The parish boundaries encompass a number of outlying Greens including:–

Almshouse Green
Birds Green
Forrey Green
High Street Green
Morris Green
Southey Green

and hamlets including:–

Cobbs Fenn
Cut Maple
Delvin End
Harrowcross
New England

The village had a number of ancient manors of which successive Lords of the principal manors were the owners of Hedingham Castle. These manors were Prayers, Greys, Grassalls (Graves Hall), Blois, Prayours Glasscocks and Hawkwoods. Another manor or large estate in the parish was Sparrows and early farms included: Baker's, Barnard's, Bloom's, Brook, Carter's, Cresswell's, Cuckoo, Egfield (Eckfield), Finch's, Hawke's Hall, Hostage's, Kentish, Pevors, Red House, Tile Kiln, Warren's, Washling's (Washlands), Webb's and Wright's. Deeks Farm was previously known as Hangmans Hall. It is interesting to note that many of these ancient names have survived into the twentieth century.

Sible Hedingham has probably been occupied since at least the Bronze Age. In 1929 some unique bronze age finds were unearthed near Tower House. Roman Pottery was found nearby and some roman brick is incorporated into the construction of Sible Hedingham Church indicating a roman settlement in the village. Mediaeval pottery and pottery kilns have been found in the village at Braintree Corner (Crows Cross) and the appropriately named Potter Street.

For many centuries, agriculture was undoubtedly the largest single employer in the village. In May, 1816 Sible Hedingham was the scene of a riot when agricultural labourers with various weapons destroyed threshing machines and other farming implements. Five young men were committed by Castle Hedingham Magistrates to the House of Correction at Halstead. Upon their arrival with Constables, four of these men were rescued by a number of Halstead residents and were at large. In the circumstances, Lewis Majendie of Hedingham Castle, ordered the Gosfield Troop of Volunteer Cavalry to assemble in Sible Hedingham until further directions from the Government.

In the Hedinghams there were once over two hundred acres of hop plantations. This crop was grown from the Tudor era until the latter half of the nineteenth century. In about 1640 in Depositions against Essex Clergymen whose livings were sequestrated, it was stated by the son of the Sible Hedingham parson that "his fathers hops were a bagging at the time they went to church in the afternoon .... and that the said hops were at Sturbridge Fair" (Stourbridge Fair near Cambridge). The hops grown in the rich, fertile ground of the Hedinghams were esteemed superior to any other in the country. These hop-yards were visited and fully described in the eighteenth century by Arthur Young. Sible Hedingham had the distinction of being the last village in Essex where hops were cultivated. Wild hops can still be found growing in several places in the village particularly along the river banks but the hop kilns have long since disappeared.

The cloth trade was one of the principal employers for some centuries until only one firm remained at the end of the eighteenth century. In the seventeenth century some Sible Hedingham woolcombers even had their own tradesmans tokens.

There was once a tannery and three maltings in Alderford Street and other maltings in Queen Street and Station Road.

Tanning was carried out in Sible Hedingham from at least the fourteenth century as Gilbert Hawkwood (the father of the famous Sir John Hawkwood) who died in 1340 was a tanner at Sible Hedingham. A tan yard was still operating in Alderford Street in the eighteenth century.

The Hedinghams had eight maltings by 1800 many of which were later owned by John Taylor of Rookwoods and then by his son Vero William Taylor, C.A., J.P. Until 1908, Vero Taylor owned the New Malting and Eleys Malting (formerly owned by Thomas Eley, a miller and merchant) at Queen Street, the Half Way House Malting at Station Road and the Home Maltings in Alderford Street (all in Sible Hedingham) as well as the Kennel Maltings at Castle Hedingham.

During the nineteenth century a number of residents were employed in the straw plaiting industry and there was one straw hat maker and a straw plait dealer. There was even a straw plaiting school at High Street Green which also taught children to read. Straw plaiting had been introduced to the area by the Marquis of Buckingham who lived at Gosfield Hall. Some of the Hedingham straw plait was sold to merchants and taken to Luton for making straw hats.

Other occupations included iron founders, tinsmiths, coopers, basket makers, toy makers and coach builders as well as the more usual blacksmiths, wheelwrights, carpenters, thatchers, bricklayers, bakers, butchers and shoemakers.

The brick making industry expanded rapidly towards the end of the nineteenth century. The earliest recorded brickworks were in existence by the 1700's at Southey Green. Following the arrival of the Colne Valley and Halstead Railway in 1861, more brickworks were established in the village. In about 1900 the industry employed about 500 men who made some seven or eight million bricks a year. The output was greater than the Colne Valley and Halstead Railway could manage and new Light Railways were proposed to connect the Hedinghams with other centres but they were never built. 'Hedingham reds' became well known and one brick maker even exported bricks to Ireland (Dublin Barracks), Egypt and Africa. Another Sible Hedingham brickmaker supplied bricks for building sixteen churches in North London.

As the brickmaking industry declined, the woodworks of Rippers gradually expanded and provided employment.

Until this century the main settlements of the village were Church Street, Alderford Street, Queen Street and Potter Street. There were very few houses in Swan Street and all the present housing estates were fields. In 1901 and 1902 over 50 building plots were advertised for sale on the "Alexandra Building Estate" and the first red brick houses were built in Alexandra Road then frequently called "New Road". In 1920 the Council Houses were built further along Alexandra Road but the actual road was not made up until 1921 after much debate.

In 1927, Cambridge Avenue was built by Frank Gibson and this was followed in 1933 by ten bungalows in Recreation Road and twenty in Gibson Road. In October, 1927, Frank Gibson handed over to Sible Hedingham Parish Council the Recreation Ground then known as Cross Path Field.

From 1924, Rippers Limited built one hundred houses in Swan Street, Brook Terrace, Station Road and Yeldham Road. Numerous dwellings were built in Swan Street and other locations and the village steadily expanded.

Some of the development and industries of the village are featured in this book. Also included are some of its former residents such as Sir John Hawkwood, the mediaeval military adventurer.

In more recent times Sible Hedingham has been the home of many interesting people including George Theodore Manning, the author of "Rural Rhymes". John Redwood-Anderson, the author and poet who lived at Lamb Cottage is buried in the village churchyard as is Major-General Sir Digby Shuttleworth, K.C.I.E., D.S.O., C.B., of Southey Green House, who was a Quarter Master General in India. His son Leiutenant Peter Shuttleworth was awarded the Military Cross in 1953 for gallantry in Korea the previous year. Colonel Charles Samman, J.P., of Bridge House was Master of the Society of Apothecaries. He had the rare distinction of being elected to this position on consecutive occasions.

A distinguished military and naval family associated with Sible Hedingham were the Fowke family who lived in Swan Street. Admiral George Fowke served in the Navy during the Napoleonic wars and lived in the village during his retirement. He was appointed an Admiral in 1825 and died in 1832. His youngest son, William Villiers Fowke, M.A., J.P. a Barrister (1818–1894) who was born in Sible Hedingham lived in Swan Street for many years before moving to Saling Grove, Great Saling where he was Lord of the Manor and Patron of the Living. Whilst living in Sible Hedingham he was Chairman of the Halstead Board of Guardians until April, 1865. His youngest son was Lieutenant General Sir George Henry Fowke (1864–1936) who was also born in Sible Hedingham. He was mentioned in despatches four times during the Boer War and held very high appointments in the British Army in France during the First World War being Adjutant General from 1916 to 1919. Sir George was created C.B., in 1915, K.C.B. in 1916 and K.C.M.G., in 1918. His sister and brother in law, Mr. & Mrs. Thomas Elrington lived in Sible Hedingham for many years at the Cedars, later named the White House in Potter Street.

Godfrey Blundell Samuelson, M.P., J.P., (1863–1941) was buried at Sible Hedingham. He had lived at Southey Green and later at Castle Hedingham before finally moving to Foxborough Hills where he died on 3rd November 1941. He was Liberal Member of Parliament for the Forest of Dean, Gloucester, from 1887 to 1892 and was Private Secretary to the Rt. Hon. A.J. Mundella (President of the Board of Trade). He was a son of Sir Bernard Samuelson, Bt., P.C., M.P., and brother of Henry Bernhard Samuelson, M.P.

Another Member of Parliament associated with Sible Hedingham was Henry Greville Montgomery, (1863–1951) who lived at Bakers Farm at about the turn of the century. He owned property and land in the village and in 1901 sold numerous building plots in Alexandra Road and Swan Street. He was Liberal Member of Parliament for Bridgewater, Somerset from 1906 to 1910 and favoured nationalization of Railways and Canals and Electoral Reform. Greville Montgomery (as he was known) was also a Newspaper Proprietor and in 1892 he founded "The British Clayworker" the organ of the Brick and Tile Trades. As a result the Institute of Clayworkers was inaugurated in 1895 and he revived the Building Trades Exhibition the same year. He was also a Past Master of the Tylers and Bricklayers Company and founded "The Brickbuilder".

During the mid nineteenth century various members of the Dillistone family owned Nurseries at Sible Hedingham and Sturmer. Sargent and John Dillistone were florists, nursery and seedsmen at Sturmer whilst William Dillistone later owned the Munro Nursery at Sible Hedingham. However it was Ezekiel Dillistone of this family who gained the distinction of raising the Sturmer Pippin apple in the 1840's.

Over one hundred years later, in 1950, Harry Claude Elsdon, who was born at Sible Hedingham, produced the Elsdon dahlia. It took him twenty years of experimenting to produce the seedling at his home in Kent. This strain has an almost black foilage with brightly coloured flowers.

Two suffragette leaders, who both suffered imprisonment for the cause, made their homes in Sible Hedingham, namely, Miss Rachel Barrett, B.Sc., and Mrs. Emily Katharine Marshall who was a devoted follower and intimate friend of Mrs. Emmeline Pankhurst. It was Emily Marshall who raised a fund to erect the statue to Mrs. Pankhurst in Westminster and persuaded Prime Minister, Stanley Baldwin, to unveil it. She was also a landscape painter of some distinction, exhibiting in the Royal Academy. She also worked hard for Hedingham Charities. Dame Christobel Pankhurst was among the many mourners at her funeral in Sible Hedingham Church in 1947. Her husband, Willoughby Marshall, was legal adviser to the Women's Social and Political Union and acted for them throughout in Civil and Criminal Court proceedings.

Another lawyer associated with the village was Henry Pigot Ireland Warburton, the well known Barrister, whose father the Rev. Henry Warburton was Rector of Sible Hedingham for the long period of 56 years. The Rev. Warburton was the author of verse published under the name of Horace Walton. He owned the living of Sible Hedingham which was understood to be one of the richest in England. His youngest son Willie George Alexander Warburton who was born in Sible Hedingham in 1860 lived in Belgium most of his life. In May, 1936 the Order of the Crown of Belgium was conferred upon him but he died the following month on 4th June, 1936 and was buried at Sible Hedingham.

The Rev. George Lister, M.A., who was Rector of Sible Hedingham from 1954 to 1958 served as a combatant in the First World War and was awarded the Military Cross and the Croce di Guerra.

Other Sible Hedingham residents who have gained distinction include Captain Fred Cornish who became a member of the National Executive Council of the British Legion. He spoke on the radio about defence during the Second World War and was mentioned in despatches. Stanley Finch of Tokat House, who was for many years a Director of Rippers Limited, became President of The British Woodwork Manufacturers Association and President of the English Joiners Association. Miss Thyra Heyworth of Hawkwood Manor was the second woman in the country to hold a driving licence.

These are only a few former residents of the village who have made noteable achievements; there are many others included in this book.

It was not only the people of the village who have sometimes hit the headlines. In 1949, a race horse called "Nimbus" won the Derby and the 2,000 guineas at Newmarket. Nimbus was owned by Mrs. Marian Glenister of Tattersall's, Sible Hedingham.

The village also claims to be the last place in England where a case of witchcraft arose. This is just one of many interesting anecdotes contained in this book.

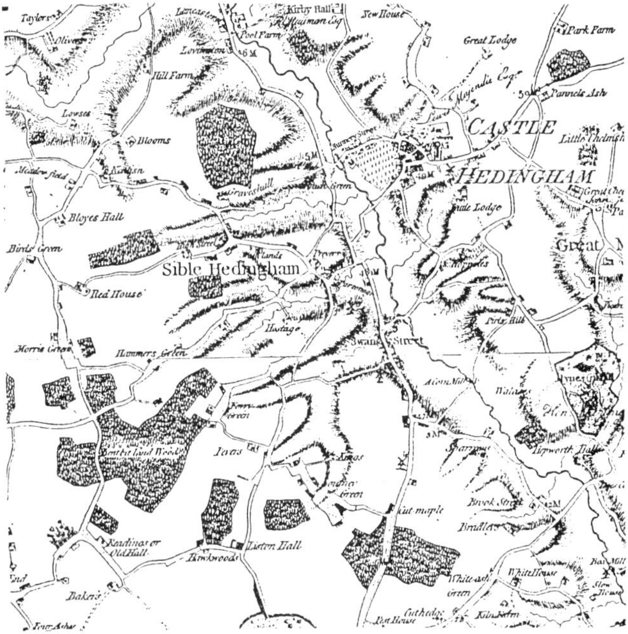

Sible Hedingham from Chapman and Andre's map of Essex, 1777.

Sible Hedingham from a map of 1891.

ST. PETERS CHURCH

The Church, dedicated to St. Peter, was mainly built during the reign of Edward III and is a fine edifice of brick and stone including some Roman tiles. The west tower, originally built C. 1340 was almost entirely rebuilt early in the 16th century when the south porch was added.

St. Peters Church and Church Street between 1890 and 1897 showing a roof on the chancel but not the nave of the church. The nave roof was replaced in 1897 at a cost of £945.

St. Peters Church before 1890 with no roof on the nave or chancel. The chancel was restored in 1890 at the sole cost of the Rev. Henry Warburton, M.A., and Mrs. Warburton. The Rev. Henry Warburton was rector here for 56 years from 1848 to 1904 being the longest serving incumbent. His father, also named Henry, was rector from 1822 to 1838. The last member of the family to hold the living was the Rev. Welby Russell Warburton, M.A., from 1904 to 1918.

The nave of the Church looking towards the Chancel and East Window. This photograph was taken in about 1930 when the church was lighted with paraffin lamps. The Hawkwood memorial can be seen in the South Aisle on the extreme right and the War Shrine in the North Aisle on the left.

Amongst the mediaeval graffiti in Sible Hedingham Church is this grotesque face, described by Sir James Laver, as a drawing of the devil. It was scratched on an octagonal column in the nave of the church and is palimpsest; the other drawing, which was probably the first one, represents a flowering branch. The devil has a fine set of teeth and two horns but otherwise his appearance does not appear evil. When this inscription was made during mediaeval times, churchgoers regarded the devil, not as a symbol of evil, but as a real person being in various guises. In some Essex villages there are stories of visits from the devil, but at Sible Hedingham there is no record of the devil actually appearing and therefore the reason for this early graffiti remains a mystery.

The oak choir stalls and on the extreme left, the priests stall, in the chancel of Sible Hedingham Church, were carved and constructed in the village by craftsmen at Rippers Limited to the design of architect, Wykeham Chancellor of Chelmsford. They were dedicated by the Bishop of Colchester on 6th March, 1929 who congratulated the parishioners upon the provision of the stalls as a beautiful addition to the ancient church. The massive oak used was of a high quality and the exquisite workmanship was a source of admiration. A large quantity of woodwork wrought by Rippers which adorn churches and other buildings are a reminder of the great wood-craftsmanship once executed in Sible and Castle Hedingham.

Sible Hedingham Church Choir in 1921.

Left to right:

Back row: George White, Cecil Goodchild (Churchwarden), Thomas Ruffle and Thomas Elrington.

Centre row: Miss Amelia Olwen Mona Evans (daughter of the Rev. Evans), William Lodge, George Webb, Norman Vagg, Frederick T. Cox, Rev. Dr. John Arthur Evans, Thomas Parsons, William Bishop (Organist), Basil Ruffle, Frank Gibson and Thomas Vagg (Verger).

Front row: Frederick Reed, Frank Headland, Jack Wiseman, ? ? , Fred North, George Rayner, ? ? , Ted Bareham, Cecil North, George Anderson, Herbert Jarvis, Thomas Redgewell, Cecil Everitt, Edward Boreham and Fred Rayner.

In August, 1916 the Sible Hedingham choir boys actually went on strike because of a proposal to introduce girls in the choir. The attitude of the boys was not supported by the men with only one man standing out. After a couple of weeks absence the boys returned but were told by the Rector, the Rev. Welby Warburton, that their services would not be required any more. The Rector was supported by practically all the adult members of the choir and during the following few weeks the singing was led by the ladies. In the course of time new boys were trained for the choir. It is interesting to note that in the above photograph taken only five years later, the choir was once again an all male choir but with a new Rector, the Rev. Dr. J.A. Evans.

A Sible Hedingham Bell Ringers outing in about 1930 on Aubrey Letch's bus which is in the background.

Back row: **Bob Young, Alfred Halls (son of Caleb Halls, the previous tower captain), Ron Rayner, John Coe, Bob Hornsby (bus driver), Harry Wiseman, Cecil Barker, Bill Cross, Bernard Pettitt, Olave Broyd.**

Front row: **Fred Wiseman, George Letch, Albert Catterwell, Pascoe Young.**

Sible Hedingham had a ring of five bells until a sixth bell was added at Michaelmas, 1912. The old tenor bell (weighing 18½ cwt.) was made by Miles Graye, 1616; the third and fifth are of dates 1627 and 1667 and the second and fourth are believed to be pre-reformation. These five bells were restored and rehung in 1912 when the new treble was added.

This bell bears the inscription:–

> "To the Glory of God, this bell, the gift of two sisters, E.A. and E. Webster, was dedicated 29th September, 1912. Think when the bells do chime it's Angel's music."

At Easter, 1914, two new treble bells (weighing 5 cwt. each) were presented to the church by the Misses Webster to complete the octave. A contemporary report stated:

> "The church now possesses one of the best peal of eight bells in the county."

The Misses Eleanor and Elizabeth Amelia Webster were great benefactors to the village. In addition to defraying the cost of some of the church bells and providing six almshouses, they also paid for various church repairs and for the upkeep of the churchyard for many years. During this time the churchyard was kept "in beautiful order" and when Elizabeth Webster died in 1920 she left £2,000 the income of which was to be devoted to maintaining and keeping in order the churchyard and approaches to the church. The Loyal Webster Lodge of Oddfellows was formed out of a Sick Benefit Club previously carried on by them. No philanthropic work was undertaken without their assistance and they never spared themselves or their money when the welfare of the people was under consideration. They were good friends to the poor and every five years they made a gift of over 80 blankets to "cottagers". It is fitting that a new road in the village had been named after them and their name will go down to posterity as two of the most generous benefactors the village has ever had. They came from a talented family. Their father James Philip Webster held an important appointment under King George III and King George IV and had apartments at Windsor Castle. Their uncle was the famous Thomas Webster (1800–1886), the Royal Academician, many of whose beautiful paintings were hung in the Royal Academy.

The Webster family lived in Swan Street for about 50 years at Hill Cottage which was renamed "The Bays" during the 1890's.

The Bays, photographed in 1947 when it was the home of Mr. & Mrs. Harry Ripper.

In 1924, the village poet, Richard Young, who was then 87 years of age wrote the following verses in memory of the Misses Webster:—

"Two ladies lived in Sible Hedingham,
We must speak in their praise;
They were the Misses Webster,
Who for years lived at "The Bays".

By the charities they used to do
Many poor families were fed;
And at the death of each of them
A great many tears were shed.

They were known to all around,
By all the local dwellers;
They gave a sum of money and banner
To the Club of the "Odd Fellows".

To the memory of their Mother dear,
And to the Glory of their God;
They built six nice almshouses
To be a free abode.

And what they have done for the church
Is too much for me to say;
The music from the lovely bells
We can hear from far away!

I hear that they have willed a sum,
I know that it is true;
To keep the churchyard in good trim
And the approaches thereunto!

Their remains lie in that churchyard,
Christian lives they had led;
Now they're lying side by side,
In their little narrow beds".

Some ten years ealier, Richard Young wrote a few lines in memory of Caleb Halls, who had been captain of the tower and who was buried in Sible Hedingham Churchyard on 10th January, 1914 aged 82 years.

"A friend of ours has passed away,
And left his friends to mourn,
He's passed the valley stream of death
And never will return;

He's bid farewell to all on earth,
He's left this world of woe,
He is not lost, but gone before,
Where you and I must go.
He was a Church Bell ringer
We always thought him head;
The ringers went and rang to him
Upon his dying bed.
His name was Mr. Caleb Halls,
They did him honour pay,
The Ringers there range muffled peals
At his burial and next day,
We hope he's joined that noble band,
Where saints and angels sing,
And play upon the golden bells,
That never cease to ring.

The above verse can still be found framed in the belfry of Sible Hedingham Church where the names of the bearers are also recorded:–

L. Wiseman	F. Wiseman	W. Clark
E. Ruffle	W. Ruffle	E. Barker

"Six brother ringers volunteered,
They all were strong and brave;
They paid their best and last respect,
They bore him to the grave".

Sible Hedingham has retained a band of bell ringers over the years and the author is grateful to the present captain, Jack Brett, for some of the above information.

Mourners at a graveside in Sible Hedingham Churchyard after a military funeral in January, 1913.

The mourners were Daniel Willett and two of his sisters Caroline and Louisa. They are standing by the grave of their brother William Willett (1833–1913) who had a military funeral. The coffin had been draped with a Union Jack and carried on a gun-carriage, drawn by six horses belonging to the 114th Battery, with the Durham Light Infantry providing an escort.

William Willett was a veteran of the Crimean War and also served in the New Zealand Expedition and the Malay War. He enlisted with the 50th Queens Own later known as the Queens Own Royal West Kent Regiment and served in the army for 21 years. The Willett family were natives of Sible Hedingham some of them being Maltsters, Farmers and Coal Merchants. Another William Willett, a nephew of the above, was buried in Sible Hedingham Churchyard in 1981 at the great age of 103 years and was probably Hedingham's oldest ever resident.

This William Willett had served in the Essex Regiment during the First World War and probably lived to be the oldest man ever to have served in that Regiment. In the few weeks preceeding February, 1922 there had been twelve burials in Sible Hedingham Churchyard and the total ages of those laid to rest amounted to no less than a thousand years, giving an average age of over 83 years. The oldest of the deceased had reached the age of 98 years and there were none younger than 75. It is noteworthy that over a century earlier, in 1817, of 21 burials, 12 were of people over 70. Sible Hedingham could certainly be described as a village whose residents lived long lives.

SIR JOHN HAWKWOOD

Sir John Hawkwood, the terror of mediaeval Italy, was born at Sible Hedingham in the 1320's, the son of Gilbert Hawkwood, a tanner. John Hawkwood entered the army of Edward III, rose in rank and was knighted after the battle of Poitiers for his bravery. After the war with France he formed and became commander of the famous "White Company" and gave notable service. The White Company was hired out to anyone who required a force of fighting men. The mercenary Hawkwood and his dauntless men-at-arms were almost continuously in demand. He fought for Pisa against Florence, for Perugia against the Pope and when his White Company was taken over by the Pope, Hawkwood fought for him. He married a niece of the Duke of Milan and settled down in Italy where he held many honours including General of the Florentine forces. He died in Florence in 1394 and was given a magnificent funeral. According to tradition King Richard II brought Hawkwood's body home, wrapped in a cloth of gold, from his tomb in the Duomo, Florence to a magnificent tomb in Sible Hedingham Church.

Although there was a memorial to him in the church, of which only the canopy remains, it is doubtful if his body was actually brought back to Hedingham. However, he was perhaps, Sible Hedingham's most famous son.

Sir John Hawkwood: A photograph of the fresco of the famous condottiere in the Duomo at Florence by Paolo Uccello in 1436.

The above print is from the "Memoirs of Sir John Hawkwood", 1782. The canopy in the south wall of the church is the only remaining fragment of the memorial to Sir John Hawkwood. It is resplendent with hawk, boar, pelican and hunting figures. On the tower of the church two bold hawks are carved as architectural puns on the family name.

The rear elevation of the former Rectory with St. Peters Church in the background. This Rectory was built with local red brick in about 1714 by the Rev. Moses Cook, M.A., who was Rector from 1690 to 1733 and founder of 'The Cook's Charity'.

In 1837, Joseph Mallord William Turner, R.A., (1775–1851), reputed to be the greatest landscape painter the world has ever known, made a water colour sketch of the Rectory with the Church in the background. The picture was truly a sketch and was never finished in detail but on the back Turner had written "Sible Hedingham Rectory, 1837". In September, 1925 a Mr. Anderson of the Anderson Galleries, New York who had owned the picture for some 30 years visited Sible Hedingham Rectory with the picture and sought the very spot where Turner must have stood to paint it. It was found that no great alteration in the Rectory had taken place. Turner was at the zenith of his fame when he visited Sible Hedingham and for over half a century produced an extraordinary succession of great pictures. The Rectory ceased to be used as such in 1961 when it was sold and is now the home of Richard Eddis, J.P., a Solicitor and one time Sible Hedingham Parish Councillor.

THE FRIENDLY SOCIETIES PARADES TO THE CHURCH

A Friendly Societies Parade entering Rectory Road from Swan Street. The photograph was taken from the Sugar Loaves Public House with Brook Farm in the background. The Brook Meadow Estate now stands on the extreme right and Bowater Rippers Limited on the left.

The Parade photographed in Church Street. The committee who arranged these parades prior to the First World War included Ernest Willis (Secretary), Eli Cornish, Harry Corder and Alfred Metson. Organisations which took part in these parades include the Sible Hedingham Band and the Loyal Webster Lodge of Oddfellows whose members included many brickmakers in the village.

These parades frequently included visiting Bands and Friendly Societies such as the Loyal Atlas Lodge of Earls Colne whose banner can be seen in the above photographs taken from Sible Hedingham Churchyard and looking along Church Street towards the former Rectory in the background.

Prior to the First World War these parades assembled in the meadow next to Bay Cottage, Swan Street. In August, 1923 the first parade since 1913 was held when those taking part met at the former Assembly Rooms in Swan Street and went to Castle Hedingham Congregational Chapel via Swan Street and Station Road. After the service the parade went to the Hedingham Castle grounds where the band played. The committee of the Loyal Webster Lodge of Oddfellows who were responsible for arranging these parades between the wars included Ernest Reginald Bayley, H.G. Britton, Frederick George Bishop, William Bishop, Bertie W. Corder, Ernest E. Gepp, William Wright Raynham, Thomas Ruffle, Robert L. Webb and C. Westrop.

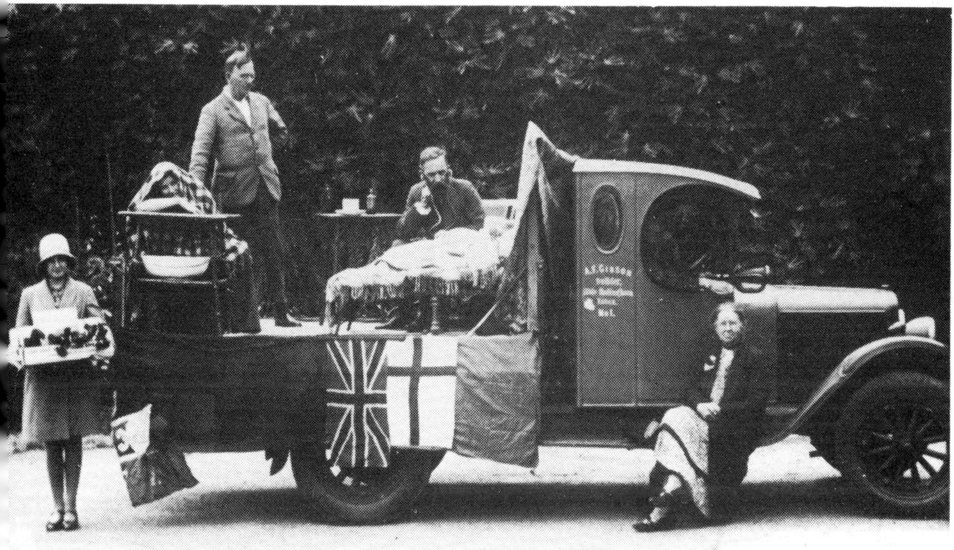

In August, 1931, the Friendly Societies and British Legion arranged a "Hospital Parade" to raise money for Hospitals and the Hedingham Nursing Association. Included in the procession were two tableaux arranged by Mrs. Ann Maria (Nannie) Twamley who is seated on the foot board of this lorry owned by Frank Gibson. In this representation of the picture "The Doctor" those taking part were Alexander Norwood Gibson (doctor), B.C. Rhodes (father), Miss Nellie Brett (mother) and Dorothy Carter (the sick child). Miss Dorothy Earey standing on the left represented the British Legion and the lorry driver was James Earey.

The other tableau depicted hospital work and included a patient being treated after an accident. The parts were taken by Nurse Ray, Robert Catterwell, Miss Joan Molecey and Tom Molecey being the victim. Miss Joyce Meadowcroft represented the British Legion and Molly Wiseman and Grace Palmer represented the Girl Guides. The above lorry was owned by George Elsdon, a village builder. The procession which included numerous Friendly Societies was accompanied by the Hedingham Brass Band and marched by way of Swan Street to the Church where a service took place.

THE BAPTIST CHURCH

In Sible Hedingham a large proportion of the population were Non-Conformists particularly during the nineteenth century. The above photograph shows a congregation standing outside the 'Old' Baptist Chapel. It was built, adjacent to the Sugar Loaves Public House, in 1807–08 to seat 500 persons.

Another Baptist Chapel, the 'New' or Rehoboth Strict Baptist Chapel was built in Swan Street and opened on 18th October, 1864. Two Hedingham men instrumental in building this chapel were John Gibson and Joseph Jay.

The present Constitutional Club in Swan Street was previously a Congregational Chapel built in 1874. An earlier chapel had been built on the same site by the Quakers in about 1813 as an 'Old Friends' Meeting House. The Quakers sold it in 1833 to the Congregationalists who were then better known as the Independents.

During the latter half of the nineteenth century there was also a chapel for the Primitive Methodists.

Of all the non-conformist chapels once in the village, only the two Baptist Chapels now survive.

'Old Baptist Sunday School' parade along Alexandra Road held during the time when Rev. James Grinnell was Minister of the Old Baptist Chapel. The Rev. Grinnell lived in one of Ethel Cottages now number 29 Alexandra Road which is the third cottage from the left above.

A Garden Party for the Baptist Church about 1930 held at Little Fields, High Street Green the home of Mr. and Mrs. George H. Mann.

Left to right, back row: Mrs. Ellis, unknown, Doris Ellis, Mrs. Lily Boreham, Rev. Rankin, Florrie Abbott, Mrs. Nellie Springett, unknown, Doris Corder, Mrs. Everitt, Mrs. Alice Corder.

Centre row: Mrs. Springett, Mrs. Tokley, Mrs. Ellen Grinnell, Rev. James Grinnell, Mrs. Mann, Reg Ellis, unknown.

Front row: Dorcas Bullard, unknown, Doris Drury (later White), Mrs. Harry Hughes, (from Halstead), ? Osborne, Ena Upchurch and Nellie Upchurch.

Sible Hedingham Primary School C. 1915

Back row: Frederick Thrower (Headmaster), Charles Watson, Frederick Everitt, ? Boreham, unknown, Stanley Wilding, ? Everitt, ? Pannell, Charles Brett, Walter Britton, Mrs. Orford (teacher).

Second row: Aubrey Bareham, ? Finch, Frank Headland, Linley Thrower, ? Daines, George Everitt, Ben Hale, unknown, John Bell, Harold Aver, William Dowe, Albert Drury.

Third row: Hubert Taylor, George Rayner, John Crysell, Horace Hale, Ambrose Wright, William Kendall, unknown, Richard Hale, William Stimson.

Front row: Jack Brett, Charles Ruffle, unknown, Charles Butler, unknown, unknown, unknown, unknown, Cecil Wilding, Maurice Everitt.

The school was built in 1840 by John Spurgeon, using local red bricks.

Standard II, Sible Hedingham Primary School, circa 1930/1931.

Back row: Jack Springett, James "Happy" Bell, Tom Bareham, Don Boreham, Don Barwood, Dick Pryke, Miss Violet Pope (later Mrs. McLuckie, schoolmistress).

Second row: Dennis Harper, Cecil Bishop, Jack Brett, Doris Ellis, Ruby Ruffle, Florence Harrod, Vic Connell, George Simpson, Doug Drury.

Front row: Phyllis Hale, Cynthia Ruffle, Kathy Latter, Freda Wiseman, Gladys Cudmore, Irene Corder, Kathy Letch, Daphne Ward.

St. Peters Primary School, Sible Hedingham, 1931.

Left to Right:

Top row: Fank Lee, ? , Russell Prouse, Sonny Goodchild, Ronald Everitt, Douglas Baggley, Gordon Bradford, Joe Cowlin, Laurie Nicholls, Stan Ruffle, Eric Mayhew, Albert Wiseman.

Second row: Mabel Bonner, Alfred Pannell, Eric Barwood, John Ruffle, Roy Harper, Spencer Rose, Gerald Clark, Roy Wilding, Kenneth Wilding, Dennis Alliston, James Plumb, John Everitt, Joan Harrod.

Third row: Iris Cock, Dorothy Pannell, Joan Noble, Fay Goodchild, ? Peacock, Beatrice Corder, Jean Taylor, Dora Kendall, Doris Letch, Hilda Weller, Gladys Ruffle, Amy Ambrose, Mrs. Kate Bishop (teacher).

Bottom row: Molly Cudmore, Peggy Cudmore, Edna Boreham, Doreen Smith, Peggy Smith, Dulcie Clarke, Jean Prouse, Molly Wilding, Mary Dyson, Nora Smith, Daisy Boreham.

Hedingham Secondary Modern School (now Hedingham Comprehensive School) was largely built in 1938. However, completion of the building was delayed because of the impending Second World War when the workmen were transferred to defence buildings. During the war the school was used as an Evacuation Centre for the London County Council and by the Ministry of Health who converted it to a Geriatric Hospital. Some school classes were held from May, 1943 for pupils from Sible Hedingham, Castle Hedingham and Great Yeldham only but it was not until 1945 that senior children from the entire catchment area were admitted and the building fully used for its intended purpose.

Hedingham Secondary Modern School Staff in 1950.
Back row: S.A. Tozer, Miss P. Jackson, H.B. Riley, D.R. Thomas, Miss E.C. Hurry, W.G. Otley, H.W. Witton, Miss E.P. Price, E. Bonner, E.G. Dyke.
Front row: F.W. Pawsey, D.F.C., R.A. Danaher, Miss D. Clark, G.C. Gardam, C. Nicholls, Mrs. D.A. Thomason, J.R. Pendle.

In the left foreground is Alderford Grange which was until 1935 the home of Dr. Henry Joseph Twamley one of the village doctors. Whilst occupied by Dr. Twamley, Alderford Grange was known as "Erinagh". During the early years of the Second World War it was occupied by James Marjoribanks, who was H.M. Vice Consul at the Foreign Office.

In 1943 Alderford Grange became the second of several "Do as you like schools" in England, the first having been established by A.S. Neill in Suffolk. The branch at Alderford Grange had a maximum limit of 24 mixed pupils boarded there including the grandaughter of Lord Bertrand Russell, O.M., (1872–1970), the English philosopher, mathematician and author. It is said that the pupils "did just what they wanted" and great relief was expressed in Sible Hedingham when the school was transferred to East Greenstead in 1950.

Alderford Grange later became the home of Mr. and Mrs. Beresford-Jones and was used as a private school by Miss Mabel Blyth. It is now the home of Dr. Norman Edwards.

Beyond Alderford Grange is the Bell Inn, Spurgeons Stores and the Almshouses and on the right Harringtons Bakery. The scene has changed very little since this photograph was taken sometime prior to 1924.

The Almshouses, Swan Street, built in 1884 by the Misses Webster of 'The Bays' in memory of their mother Maria Webster who had died in 1882. There were originally six almshouses built "for the accommodation of six aged women" but in 1985 they were converted into four, the work being carried out by A.H.P. Builders Limited.

A view down Spurgeons Hill (Swan Street) before the road was made up in 1908. The almshouses are near the centre next to Spurgeons Stores and on the right is Hill House.

Church Street with St. Peters Church in the background sometime between 1897 and 1904. The photograph can be so dated because the church is shown with its new roof which was completed in 1897. In 1904 two red brick cottages were erected next to the White Horse Inn which were not built when this photograph was taken. Note the unmade road and the children posing for the cameraman which was often a feature of the period.

The junction of Church Street and Alexandra Road with an old cottage which was demolished sometime after the Second World War. This cottage was occupied by the Smith family and the man standing in front of the cottage is Jim Smith.

Church Street in about 1900 with a man bearing a yoke and two pails, presumably carrying water. The shop on the left is Walter "Porky" Ruffle's Pork Butchers shop which was in existence prior to the First World War. It was in Church Street where the Hedingham Toy Works were situated, between the White Lion (on the right of this photograph) and the stream.

Until about 1900 the making of childrens toys in the village was quite a flourishing industry. It was introduced to Sible Hedingham prior to 1850 by Edward Everton, a wood turner from London and taken up by the Wiseman family including William, Arthur and Lewis Wiseman, the latter starting work as a half-timer in the business and later becoming a painter and decorator. From Sible Hedingham large consignments of whip tops, peg tops, handles for skipping ropes, vases and wooden egg cups were despatched three or four times a week to wholesale houses in London and Birmingham. In addition to providing a demand for local labour this business also served as an outlet for home grown timber, ash and birch poles being very suitable for the work. Maple wood and willow were also used, the latter coming from the Hedingham Willow Grounds which yielded much material for the toy works. Church Street was frequently blocked with loads of timber, there being as many as five carriages at a time waiting to be unloaded. John Kendall of Church Street and Charles Butler of Swan Street carried on a prosperous trade in selling and carting the poles. Considerable labour was also employed during the summer months in peeling the poles ready for use. All the lathes had to be treadled or turned by hand which was very laborious work and goods were produced by the gouge and chisel which were the principal tools. Foreign competition was the cause of the industry's downfall but the Wiseman family stuck to it with great pertinacity accepting other work in the day time and keeping up the toy trade in the evening. Shortly after the outbreak of the First World War in 1914 the question was raised, "Did Germany steal Hedingham Toy Trade?"

Church Street looking towards School Hill in Edwardian days. The 'Little Wonder' shop now stands on the site of the former barn building (in the centre) which was then owned by Frank Mead. Note the number of people who have turned out to watch the photographer, a rare sight in those days.

Swan Street with the former Post Office and Public Telephone on the right and beyond that the Bell Public House of which successive members of the Harrington family were licensees for many years. The Assembly Rooms once stood behind the second cottage on the left.

Swan Street in about 1927. The white weatherboarded building was once used as a printing works. The ground floor was later converted into two shops; one being Norman McLeods gents' outfitters with a hairdressing saloon at the rear and the other was let to Donald David Copsey, a fishmonger and fruiterer. The first floor was a hall used by numerous organisations including the Hedingham Brass Band, the Hedingham Labour Party, the Women's Co-operative Guild, the Amalgamated Society of Woodworkers, the Machinists, the Woodworkers and two Labourers Unions. On 1st May, 1938 this building was razed to the ground by a serious fire which also damaged nearby property including the adjoining Hedingham Nursery where fencing and plants suffered and Bob Barrett's blacksmiths shop at the rear.

The small 'lean to' shop near the centre of the photograph has had many uses over the years including a butchers, grocers, photographers and was once the village library until the new library was built on the site of the former fire station opposite Brook House.

Swan Street about 1912 showing A.F. Gibson's builders yard and his residence 'Oakdene' the construction of which was completed in March, 1910. In the background is 'Eden House' and the 'Adam and Eve' yard owned by another former builder; George Elsdon. Cambridge Avenue and several houses, bungalows, Don Earey's butchers shop and Barclays Bank now stand between these former builders yards. The hand cart in the road is believed to be that of Henry Jaggard who was a Baker in Potter Street for many years and who used a cart for delivering his bread.

Alderford Street in 1895 with Alderford Mill in the background. The name 'Alderford' has existed in various forms since the Domesday Book of 1086 when it was recorded as 'Alreforda'. The Court Rolls of 1530 record it as 'Alderforde strete alias Aldermanstrete' and references to 'Alderford Myll' appear from 1547. However during the greater part of the nineteenth century Alderford Street was known as Watermill Lane. Alderford House with the double bow windows was the home of Dr. Sidney Thorp, M.R.C.S., during the latter half of the nineteenth century and it is interesting to note that it is again the home of a Doctor namely Dr. Irene Bainbridge. At the end of the eighteenth century there was a woolcombing factory at the rear of Alderford House owned by James Finch who was also a hop merchant. The woolcombing trade was mainly concerned with the weaving of a rough woollen cloth called Bay and Say. Nathaniel Long was the Say-scourer and in 1785 John Spurgeon, the son of Clement Spurgeon a Halstead Apothecary came to Sible Hedingham to learn the art of woolcombing. His indentures stated that his apprenticeship to the trade was to be for seven years without pay! He later became foreman at the factory and in 1823 was appointed village constable to keep law and order in Sible Hedingham.

New England, between the wars, when Alderford Hill was still an unmade road. The weather-boarded cottage on the left was for many years the home of Albert Redgewell but the thatched cottage in front has long since been demolished. It is understood that this group of cottages known as New England was so named because it was 'over the water', in other words on the other side of the River Colne to the remainder of Sible Hedingham in the same way that New England, U.S.A. is across the Atlantic Ocean from England. At one time the River Colne was crossed at Alderford Street by a ford before the bridge was built.

Sugar Loaves Lane (now Rectory Road) between the Sugar Loaves Public House and Grays Hall as it was about 1900. The scene is very different today with the Brook Meadow estate on the left and the Sugar Loaves estate on the right.

The former Y.M.C.A. hut in Alexandra Road now the site of Parkfields Flats and the house known as 'Baytos'. The houses beyond are Council Houses built by the former Halstead Rural District Council shortly after the First World War. The Y.M.C.A. hut originally stood upon Braintree Fairfield and had been given to Braintree by George Courtauld, M.P., J.P., (1830–1920) at a cost approaching £1,000. In 1925 it was dismantled and moved to Sible Hedingham where it was re-erected to serve as a village club. The work was carried out by Frank Gibson from whom the site was acquired. The hut remained the property of the Y.M.C.A. and was run under its rules. The formal opening took place on 21st January, 1926 when Sir Arthur Yapp, K.B.E., the General Secretary of the Y.M.C.A. gave an address. The actual opening was performed by Miss Sparrow of Rookwoods whose brother Col. Richard Sparrow was Chairman of the organising committee. During the Second World War the hut was used extensively for providing food and refreshments for servicemen who were stationed in the vicinity. Sometime after the war the hut was removed and Parkfields flats now occupy the site. Bert Corder built the house to the right of the hut known as 'Baytos' and his builders yard was situated at the rear. The car in the above photograph is believed to be that of Dr. P.W. Putnam who then lived in Alexandra Road.

Rookwoods Mansion was built about the middle of the eighteenth century and later became the home of the Taylor family including John Taylor (a maltster, farmer and landowner) who was father of Vero William Taylor, J.P., C.A. Rookwoods was later occupied by Ulick Burke (an eminent London Barrister who was one of the first Trustees of Halstead Cottage Hospital), Mark Gentry (a Master Brickmaker and one of Sible Hedinghams largest employers) and Colonel Richard Sparrow, C.M.G., D.S.O., F.R.G.S., F.Z.S., J.P., who had a distinguished career in the 7th Dragoon Guards.

Kimberley Lodge, Swan Street with its owner John Sidey Stuart who was a Churchwarden at Sible Hedingham. He spent some time in Kimberley, South Africa and on his demise the property was left to his daughters the Misses Stuart. The property then passed to Miss Caroline Corder who later built Kimberley Bungalow adjacent. Kimberley Lodge was renamed Appletree Lodge by a more recent owner.

An early photograph of the late tudor Bakers Farm House, off Lamb Lane.

This interesting house, often recorded as 'Baykers' was the home of numerous people over the years including Edward Killingworth Johnson, R.W.S., Colonel George Malcolm, Greville Montgomery, John Smith, Isaac Audus, Captain Robert Johnstone, O.B.E., William Allingham and George Howell. 'Baykers' had been in the occupation of Edward Johnson's family for over three hundred years. He was an artist and a member of the Royal Society of Painters in Water-colours. When he died in 1896 he was buried in Sible Hedingham Churchyard.

Margery Louise Allingham (1904–1966) who stayed at 'Baykers' in her young days, was a detective story writer and created the gentle detective Albert Campion. She published thirty novels but it was not until her death on 30th June, 1966 that her delightful lighthearted tales of Essex village life were discovered. She was the elder daughter of Herbert John and Emily Jane Allingham and married Philip Youngman-Carter, an artist, in 1927. She lived on the edge of the Essex salt marshes and from 1934 at d'Arcy House, Tolleshunt d'Arcy. Her father who died in 1936 was editor of the 'London Journal' and the 'Christian Globe'. It was his brother, William Allingham, who actually lived at 'Baykers'.

In 1919, Richard Young wrote a poem titled "Aeroplane Descent" about Lieut. E. Allingham of the Royal Air Force who lived at Bakers Farm.

On Empire Day at Sible Hedingham,
Our hearts were filled with joys;
An Aeroplane came to the ground,
Which pleased the girls and boys.

The Airman he was Mr. Allingham,
The day was bright and calm;
He visited his parents,
Who live at Bakers Farm.

His parents they were overjoyed,
By the visit he did pay;
His presence gave them cause to wish,
That he could longer stay.

He took a very little flight,
A lady friend he took;
It was a pretty sight to see him
When he looped the loop.

Later on he took his farewell flight,
They bid us all adieu;
They waved their hands and said goodbye,
Goodbye to me and you.

'Willowbrooke', Station Road was built for W. Charlton Ripper with 'Hedingham reds' in 1905. The interior of this house contains some fine wooden pannelling and doors. It was later the home of Dr. Richard Allen and currently of Mr. David Colthorpe.

The former Police House in Potter Street, now the home of Iris and Alfred Ruffle. Standing in the garden is Sergeant Chapman of the County Police. The house has changed very little since this photograph was taken in the early Edwardian era. The house was built in 1831 and was for many years owned by members of the Spurgeon family.

One well remembered Sible Hedingham Policeman was Sergeant William Mower who retired in 1903 and lived at Colne Cottage, Swan Street. By 1945, when he was 92 years of age, he was the oldest pensioner from the Essex Constabulary in which he had served for over 30 years and had been a police pensioner over 40 years. He also held the distinction of being the oldest Bee Keeper in Essex.

A horse and tumbril belonging to T. Bradridge & Co., coal and corn merchants photographed outside the former Maltings Cottages, off Station Road. The man standing in front of the tumbril is Benjamin Smith of Crouch Green, Castle Hedingham. Beyond the cottage was a maltings owned by T. Bradridge & Co., now the site of Rippers Woodworks in Station Road.

T. BRADRIDGE & Co., Ltd.

"The Firm for Value"

Corn & Coal Merchants, Seed Growers and Maltsters, Poultry & Dog Food Specialists

Poultry Appliances, Bird Seeds, Farm and Garden Seeds, etc. always kept in stock.

Best Quality our Speciality. *Try our Coals for Quality and Economy.*

Depôts at—

Halstead, Hedingham, Yeldham, etc., Essex

Advertisement dated 1922

Swan Street before the first tarmacadam surface was laid in 1908 and the cottages on the left demolished. On the right were Spurgeons Stores and Sible Hedingham Post Office. The Post Office moved to its present site in 1928 but the Stores continued under the ownership of 'Ned' (Edgar) and 'Arkie' (Alfred) Spurgeon until they retired in 1967.

John Spurgeon standing in front of his grocery and drapery stores in Swan Street which was also the Post Office and Telephone exchange.

John Spurgeon was a Registrar of Marriages from 1873 to 1917 having succeeded his father Joseph Steward Spurgeon who had been Registrar since 1842. It was Joseph Spurgeon who established the shop in 1824 and was postmaster of Sible Hedingham from 1860 to 1892. His son John was postmaster from 1892 until 1928 when the post office was transferred to its present location further along Swan Street. However postage stamps could still be purchased from Spurgeons Stores until its closure in 1967. Joseph Spurgeon had succeeded William White as postmaster in 1860. William White was a Blacksmith who ran the earlier post office in conjunction with his forge almost opposite the Alderford Street junction with Swan Street. It was said that William White was so annoyed at having to leave his anvil so often to sell penny stamps that he resigned after a short time. There was then only one delivery and one despatch of letters each day, the letters arriving by mail cart. One of Joseph Spurgeons predecessors was heard to speak of a heavy mail one day which consisted of 13 letters! The telegraph service was installed in Sible Hedingham in 1888 and the first message was sent by Dr. Sidney Thorp who was in practice in the village and lived at Alderford House, the second telegram being sent by Mark Gentry, the brickmaker. Spurgeons Stores which was latterly managed by brothers, Ned and Arkie (Edgar and Alfred) was in existence over 140 years. In the early days the business was styled as "Drapers, Hatters and Undertakers" and over the years evolved into "Grocers, Drapers and Outfitters". It was frequently stated by many people "You can buy anything at Spurgeons".

The Hedingham Spurgeons were relations of the Rev. Charles Haddon Spurgeon (1834–1892) who was said to have been England's Greatest Preacher. He sometimes visited his relations in Hedingham whilst on route to and from the nearby village of Stambourne where his grandfather, the Rev. James Spurgeon, had been minister of the Congregational Chapel for the long period of 54 years from 1810 to 1864.

Sweet Shop and cottage at Church Street, Sible Hedingham. Occupied by Mr. and Mrs. Oscar Brett who are standing on the right.

A familiar scene in Sible Hedingham and surrounding villages for many years was Henry Baines of Castle Hedingham with his pony and cart, used for collecting orders and delivering merchandise for his Grocery and Drapery shops. This photograph, taken about 1913 outside the cottage in Church Street, Sible Hedingham (now occupied by Jack Brett) shows Henry Baines (holding case) with young Norman Vagg on the cart.

In 1890, Henry and James Baines took over the grocery and drapery business in Castle Hedingham known as "Castle Stores" from William Hart. In 1919, Harold and Cyril Baines joined the firm and James retired. The firm had another grocery shop in Potter Street, Sible Hedingham which unfortunately closed during the Second World War owing to staff difficulties. Their third shop in Wethersfield continued until 1963 when Harold and Cyril Baines retired.

The former Grocers shop at Church Street which was owned by the Carter family who also owned the Grocers shop in Alderford Street. Standing in front is George Hale.

An early view of the shop at High Street Green owned by Ernest and Minnie Wilding.

PUBLIC HOUSES, HOTELS, INNS AND TAVERNS

A number of poems relating to Sible Hedingham and particularly the passing away of a resident of the village or other occurence of local interest, were written by Richard Young. He was born in the village, living in Swan Street and died in 1927 at the age of 90 years. Another poet associated with the village was John Redwood-Anderson, who lived at Lamb Cottage and was President of the Essex Poetry and Prose Society.

A poem or ballad relating to the village inns has survived in various versions and may have been written by Richard Young. Two of the versions are as follows:–

"The Windmill sails went round and round,
The Half Moon shone upon the ground,
The Black Horse kicked the Lamb which made the Bell to ring,
The Swan went swimming down the stream, the Bird in Hand did sing,
The Sugar Loaves they were so sweet it made the Lion roar,
Which frightened the White Horse into the Carpenters Arms and did'nt shut the door."

"The east wind turned the Windmill round,
The Half Moon shone upon the ground,
The Black Horse kicked the quiet Lamb
which caused the Bell to ring,
The Swan went swimming down the stream
and the Bird in Hand did sing,
The Sugar Loaves took a fright
which made the Lion roar,
The White Horse ran into the Carpenters Arms
and forgot to shut the door.
Bottle Hall's nothin' at all."

Several of these public houses are referred to and illustrated in the next few pages. Of the remainder, the Bird in Hand stood in Swan Street about half way between the Swan Inn and Hilton House. It was later converted to a private house named "Braeside" and stood on the Hilton House side of the former Forge House. Braeside, Forge House and other cottages were demolished about twenty years ago.

The Carpenters Arms, which had previously been called 'The Joiners Arms' later became the Hen and Chickens and was at High Street Green. As the Joiners Arms, the landlords were Frederick George Coult who was a Carpenter and Walter Elsdon, a builder. John Smith, a thatcher, was later landlord of the Carpenters Arms for some twenty years.

The Windmill was on the brow of the hill between Braintree Corner and Cut Maple. The first beer retailer recorded at the Windmill was Edward Conway. He was succeeded by Henry Metson who was landlord for the long period of 35 years until his death in 1932. Henry Metson was also the miller of the nearby post windmill and his father, Charles Metson, worked the water mill, later known as Hovis Mill.

The former Half Moon Public House in Queen Street, photographed before its restoration.

It was probably built early in the 16th century on a half-H-shaped plan with the south west wing being added in the 17th century. The landlords were successive members of the Finch family who originated from Gestingthorpe. Arthur Finch held the licence for over 60 years taking it over when he was 20 years of age and retaining it until his death in 1938 at the age of 81 years. During this time he had an unblemished record never having to appear before the magistrates for any contravention of the licensing laws. Arthur Finch also farmed Warrens Farm at Southey Green in succession to William Corder. In 1938, Ernest Finch who was a very keen Gardener and a son of Arthur Finch became Landlord for the final few years until its closure in 1958.

In 1973, permission was given for the old Half Moon to be dismantled, moved away from the road and reconstructed to retain its character. The proposed move never took place and the building was later restored.

Potter Street in about 1895 with the former Grocery shop owned by the Baines family on the left. In the centre was the Black Horse Public House which later became the 'Royal Coffee Rooms' and now commonly known as the 'Coffee House'. The cottages on the right have long since been demolished and replaced with the 'Dolls House'.

The landlords of the Black Horse included Bartholomew Brown, John King, John Root, Thomas Kendall, William Butler, Isaac Steward who was also a higgler, Mark Partridge and Mrs. Emmeline Partridge. In the eighteenth century there were Strawberry Gardens at the rear of the Black Horse .... "where Gentlemen and ladies were accommodated with Red and White Ports, as neat as imported, ...".

This house now known as "Swaynes" at the corner of Potter Street and Lamb Lane was formerly 'The Lamb Inn'. Early landlords were William Jaggard, Ware Stephenson, William Butler and Robert Prentice who also carried on the business of a wheelwright. They were succeeded by Samuel Watkinson, William Mayhew, James Coe and Jeffrey Mayn. Jeffrey Mayn was an accountant and registrar of births and deaths who later moved to a cottage in Swan Street (now 31 Swan Street). The Lamb was later occupied by the Kendall family and adjacent buildings were used by John and Richard Kendall who were carting contractors, coal and forage merchants, farmers, hurdle makers, timber merchants, furniture removers and job masters. This photograph taken during the early 1900's shows three horses and traps owned by John and his son Richard Kendall. John Kendall was born in Sible Hedingham in 1827 and by 1920 when he was 93 years old he was the oldest resident in the village. He resided at the old Lamb for 30 years and farmed Bakers Farm for a similar period.

The Bell Inn, Swan Street which is over 300 years old photographed before the new brick facade was placed over the ground floor in about 1900.

Landlords of the Bell over the years have included George Bird, David Simpson, William Digby, Charles Roast, Norval Dobson Hunt, Arthur Gray, Frederick Partridge Smerdon, Mrs. Rose Harrington and Miss Lilian Harrington.

The Bell Inn is said to possess two ghosts. A very cold bedroom is apparently haunted by the ghost of a sixteen year old girl with long black hair. Apparently the girl had used the room in her lifetime and having been happy in it wished to say there. The other ghost is said to be of a little old man who knocks on a downstairs door in the night. This may all be fiction but one fact associated with the Bell Inn is that one landlady, namely Mrs. Rose Harrington became not only the oldest lady ever to hold a licence in England but also held a license for more years than any other. She had held the license for 66 consecutive years when she died at the age of 92 years in 1960. In May 1949 the Directors of Greene King Limited, the Brewers, had presented her with a clock on the completion of over 50 years as tenant of the Bell. Her record was unique.

The Swan Inn, Swan Street about 1930 when the landlord was William Farrant.

He was landlord for 40 years until succeeded by William Armriding. Earlier landlords included Isaac Hubbard, Charles Rallings, Joseph Dove, who was also a colt breaker, Alfred George Foster, William Toswell, George Toswell, also a nurseryman, Mrs. Evangeline Toswell, Cornelius James Brundle and Anthony Lewis.

Until 1975 the Public House only occupied the left of the building and on the right was a private residence known as 'Swan Cottage' which was occupied by Fred Corder when this photograph was taken. Harringtons Bakery (previously a Butchers shop) is to the left of the Swan and the cottages beyond the Bakery on the very edge of the road have long since been demolished. The Swan Inn was built in the 15th century and the front refaced with brick in 1809. It was in 1863 that what is claimed to be the last case of Witchcraft in England emanated from the Swan Inn. A man known as "Dummy" who was in his 80's and believed to be of French origin frequented the Inn. He lived in a "lonely hovel" in New England (an area beyond Alderford Mill) and apparently had his tongue cut out by the Chinese when captured by them whilst fighting for the French. As a consequence he could not talk but only make strange noises in his throat. He was also said to be "a little queer in the head" and would wear all the clothes he had given to him and was frequently seen with four hats on his head.

One night he called at a beer shop in Ridgewell seeking lodgings and was refused. He made unpleasant noises in his throat to show his displeasure and made off. His utterances were interpreted as a curse and when Emma Smith, the beer house keeper afterwards became ill poor old Dummy got the blame. On 3rd August, 1863, Emma Smith in high dudgeon discovered Dummy in the tap room of the Swan. She demanded that he return to Ridgewell to break his evil spell but he refused, fearing that his throat would be cut. A row ensued and when they left the Swan with a mob of drunken men, Emma Smith pushed Dummy into the stream in Water Mill Lane (now Alderford Street) which was then much deeper and wider than it is now. Emma Smith decided to put the charge of witchcraft to the test. If he swam he was guilty and if he sank he was innocent. Emma Smith and Samuel Stammers, a Sible Hedingham carpenter, threw Dummy into the stream again and again until it became obvious that he was in danger of drowning when Stammers pulled him clear. He was left exhausted in his drenched clothes and a month later died in the Workhouse. "Emma Smith, the witch hunting beer house keeper from Ridgewell and Samuel Stammers, the drunken skylarking carpenter of Sible Hedingham each received six months hard labour for their part in causing his death". Could this last known case of witchcraft in England be one of Sible Hedingham's main claims to fame?

'The Sugar Loaves Inn' also known as 'The Three Sugar Loaves' or 'Ye Olde Sugar Loaves' was built about 1600.

It is a timber framed building which for many years had been plastered over. The landlords have included Thomas Smith, William Root, Daniel Root, Woodford Weybrew, Thomas Kendal, Thomas Taylor, John Foreman, Robert Brett (also a brick-layer), John Perry (a timber merchant and farmer), John Drury, Frederick Metson, Robert Lewis Webb, Ernest Pailthorpe, Thomas Martin Lindsell and Oliver Roberts.

Of all these landlords perhaps Thomas Martin Lindsell, who is on the above photograph with his wife and son, was the most outstanding. He was a Freeman of the City of London and the World's Champion Typist, commended by King Edward VII. He was first to conceive the idea of picture drawing on the typewriter.

Until early in the twentieth century the village stocks stood outside 'The Three Sugar Loaves' which has been so named for at least two hundred years as it is mentioned in a Chelmsford Chronicle advertisement of the 9th March, 1787.

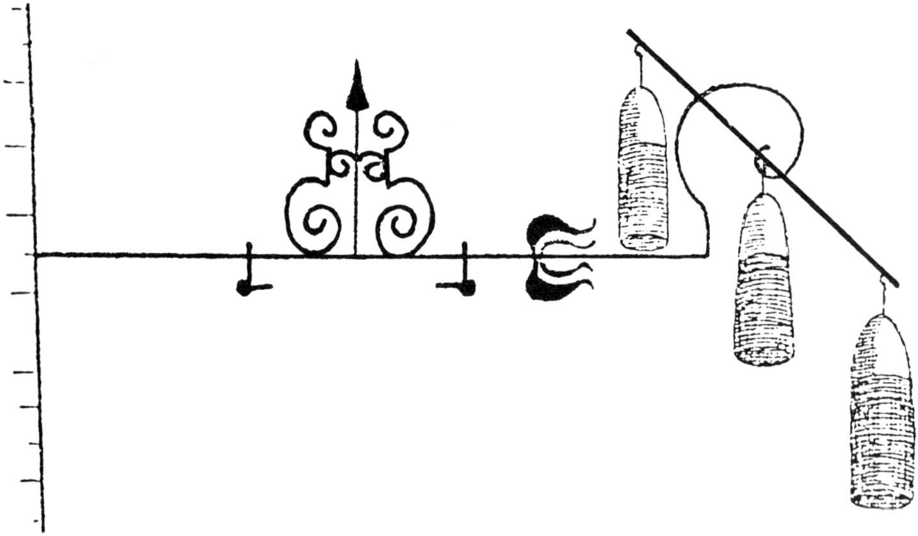

This sketch of 'The Three Sugar Loaves' is of the bracket which held the sign and is also featured in the above photograph.

An early view of Church Street with the Church in the background. On the extreme right was Carters shop and beyond that the White Lion Inn.

The White Lion had numerous landlords over the years including John Orbell who was also a carpenter, John Coe, William Richard Slee, William J. Frostick, Harry Martin Sharpe, Percy James Howes and William Eldridge. The White Lion Inn which was built about the end of the 15th century is said to have been the old Poor House.

Sible Hedingham also had a Pest House, for smallpox cases, which was situated at the far end of Lamb Lane near the junction of Watery Lane and Sandy Lane. This Pest House, which was in existence during the 1820's and 1830's, was most suitably located being in an isolated position.

During 1914 and 1915 a smallpox hospital was built at "Collyers" (now Oak House) near the crossroads to Wethersfield and Blackmore End. This hospital was also in an isolated position and provided accommodation for cases of smallpox arising in North West Essex. It closed sometime prior to the Second World War.

The White Horse Public House and adjacent Butchers shop at Church Street, which was largely built in the 15th century.

Several landlords carried on the butchers shop and a brewery in conjunction with the Inn including John Fitch, Richard Fitch, Frederick Clarke and Sarah Clarke. The Brewery at the rear of the White Horse consumed 500 sacks of malt annually. Later landlords were Harry Youngs who continued the butchers shop, John Drury who was also a farmer, William J. Drury and Mrs. Alice Stow.

Bottle Hall Public House and Blacksmiths shop photographed prior to the First World War when William Smith was the blacksmith and beer retailer.

In 1901 he succeeded Thomas Smith in both trades which he continued simultaneously until his death in 1927, when Philip Charles Smith became proprietor of the public house. The Smith family were prominent in the shoeing and blacksmith industry in the Hedinghams and surrounding district for many years. William Smith had been a blacksmith at Gainsford End, Toppesfield before returning to Bottle Hall in 1901. The Smith family had been at Bottle Hall earlier. Lewis Thomas Newman White Smith and Mrs. Susan Smith had resided there for nearly 50 years when they sold it in 1889.

William John White and Mrs. Susannah White then went into occupation as both beer retailers and blacksmiths until James William Clark purchased the property in 1896. Within the next five years the Smith family had returned to Bottle Hall.

A feature of this appropriately named public house, are the bottles built into the walls and windows as shown on the left of this photograph.

Cut Maple Post Windmill prior to 1915 with Henry Metson its last miller.

The first recorded owner was Micah Corder (1712–1782) who left it to his widow Anna Corder (1738–1810) during her life and upon her decease it was bequeathed to their son Joseph Corder (1769–1840). Thomas Legerton owned the mill until his death in 1845 and was succeeded by Fred and Horace Legerton. Sometime during the early 1850's the mill was moved on rollers some 50 yards when Charles Metson became the owner.

A later view of Cut Maple Windmill which had ceased work in 1915.

The mill was to sadly deteriorate even further before it was finally demolished in 1956. The Metson family also farmed the surrounding land and owned the former Windmill Public House nearby.

Tower Windmill, Lamb Lane was built with 900,000 local red bricks in 1825 by bricklayer, John Brett for miller, Richard Fitch. A post mill (which was blown down) previously stood on this site the millers of which were Edmund Bunn until 1792, John Kemp who was made bankrupt in 1817 and Joseph Legerton. This handsome tower mill was built and fitted up regardless of expense which presumably led to the bankruptcy of Richard Fitch four years later.

The tower windmill was owned by successive members of the Eley family from 1829 namely Robert, John and Thomas respectively. They were followed by the Metson family and the mill was last used by Arthur Metson in 1916 by which time an auxiliary steam engine was used if there was insufficient wind. This splendid example of a tower mill was sadly demolished in August 1923 by William Harry Eade and the materials reused. There were many pieces of fine old oak the weight of which amounted to about 25 tons. Some of the timbers had come from the earlier post mill.

Alderford Mill, Alderford Street in about 1925 with the house occupied by Frederick George Bishop, the miller, on the right.

He was also an agricultural and electrical engineer, haulier, threshing contractor and corn merchant. In 1922 he inaugurated an electric supply to about fifty houses and business premises in the village using his own generators. In February, 1933, his electric generating station was destroyed by fire but he was soon able to supply his customers with electric current again. When the grid system reached Sible Hedingham his supply was compulsorily taken over by the old East Anglian Electricity Supply Company.

Alderford Watermill, Alderford Street when in the ownership of Frederick George Bishop. The mill has been owned by the Rawlinson family since 1926. They ground wholemeal flour until the Second World War and after that animal feeds. It is one of the best preserved watermills in Essex and contains six stones.

An early view of Hulls Watermill on the River Colne. The chimney on the right has long since been demolished. This watermill is more commonly known as 'Hovis Mill' having been owned by Hovis Limited and has more recently become known as 'Maplestead Mill'. Although the mill is within the Great Maplestead parish boundary, being on the Maplestead side of the river, it is regarded by many as being in Sible Hedingham.

Hull's Mill, so named since at least 1625 until early this century when it was still described as 'Hull's Roller Mills'. During the latter half of the nineteenth century it was owned by the Metson family. Following the First World War it was acquired by Hovis Limited when an engine was installed for flour milling but water power was still used for grinding corn. When it closed in 1957 it was one of the last small country flour mills. During the majority of the time it was owned by Hovis, the mill was managed by Henry Noble and his son John, who lived in the Mill House shown on the right of the above photograph.
(Photograph courtesy of the Museum of the Working Horse, Toppesfield).

Sible Hedingham, looking over the River Colne, whilst in flood, towards Castle Hedingham. The river marks the boundary between the two Hedinghams. The three-arch red brick bridge over the river was described as a very substantial one when it was built to connect Sible and Castle Hedingham in 1736. It is therefore the oldest surviving bridge over the Colne and like so many other bridges it replaced a ford. There is an inscription on the keystone on its downstream (south) side "Robert Poole, surveyor, 1736". Poole was a Hedingham man and had been employed some years earlier as county surveyor but this was not a county bridge. It was built at the instigation of the then owner of Hedingham Castle who raised £60 and persuaded the Vestry to vote £210 and finally extracted from the Turnpike Trust, which maintained the approach roads, a further £210 'as a mere donation'. This bridge was enlarged in 1819 and this is recorded by a stone on the north side.

Fields adjacent to the River Colne in Sible and Castle Hedingham were used for Osier growing. The field pictured above was in Sible Hedingham opposite the former railway station.

The principal osier growers were the Westrop family of Castle Hedingham who had another osier ground in Nunnery Street. Osier growing and peeling was carried out by Samuel Westrop and later by Arthur and Harry Westrop. In Sible Hedingham Harry Westrop grew osiers on six acres of land and employed twenty hands for peeling. Soon after the First World War an unknown blight ruined the entire crop and he had to seek other employment. The rods, after peeling, were bundled for despatch by rail mainly to London but some were used locally by basket makers. Early basket makers in Sible Hedingham included Horace Dodman and James Goss. As late as 1927 Hovis Limited who owned Hulls Mill were advertising for osier peelers for their osier bed near the mill which presumably had not been troubled by the blight further along the river. Hulls Mill Osier Bed together with the remainder of Hulls Mill Farm was advertised for sale by Hovis Limited in 1938 but not sold. Osiers were still being cut by Sam Turner at Hulls Mill Osier Bed until the early years of the Second World War.

The Blacksmiths, Swan Street prior to 1914 when Bert White was the Blacksmith. He enlisted into the army during the First World War but never returned home. Left to Right: Two employees of Bert White, one of whom was Noah Kendall, Bert White with his son George White, Fred North, Harold North, three unknown and William Gatwood on horseback who was employed by Charles Halsey at Bridge House. This blacksmiths was almost opposite the Alderford Street junction with Swan Street. It is interesting to note that in the 1830's Sible Hedingham had a woman blacksmith namely Ann Rudd. One of the last blacksmiths in the village was Bob Barrett of Swan Street who died in 1952.

Gibson's Garage, Swan Street, circa 1930, with two employees: Harry Smith and Thomas Redgewell. Hubert Gibson started repairing cars in 1919 in a shed at the rear of his father's builders yard and the following year rented the above garage from Lewis Wiseman who had purchased it from Mark Gentry in 1917. Ned Spurgeon was in partnership with Hubert Gibson until 1925 and in 1927 Hubert Gibson acquired the property from Lewis Wiseman. The original petrol pumps were worked by hand and a cycle and wireless works also existed on the site under the same ownership. Hubert Gibson continued the business for some 45 years until he sold it in 1965.

In 1941 George Roy Tanner commenced bottling and delivering milk from "Chapmans" Farm (Alderford Farm) and five years later built this processing and bottling plant at Oxford Lane. (Photographed 1973.) The dairy has gradually expanded over the years and milk is now delivered in four counties and employment found for about one hundred people.

THE BRICK, TILE, POTTERY AND DRAIN PIPE MAKING INDUSTRY

An engine and trucks used during the early 1900's to haul clay from pits on one side of Wethersfield Road, Sible Hedingham across the road to the Langthorne Brick Works which were owned by Mark Gentry. The driver of the engine was 'Bunny' Beadle and two of the other men on the photograph are Herbert 'Swagger' Wiseman and Harry 'Higgler' Broyd.

The engine known as 'Tin Pot' with driver 'Bunny' Beadle.

The Brick, Tile and Pottery Works at Southey Green, Sible Hedingham prior to the First World War showing the cottages built by William Corder. Left to Right: William Bruty, John Corder, Fred Corder, Harry Corder (three brothers), Henry Corder and another John Corder (cousins). This photograph shows the top of the old kiln on the bottom left hand corner and a variety of the pottery, pipes, bricks and tiles made here.

The later Scotch up-draught kiln being fired at the Southey Green Brick, Tile and Pottery works. Southey Green, Sible Hedingham in 1937 showing Harry Corder (owner, on top of the kiln) and his brother Fred Corder standing below. Harry Corder was on top of the kiln to control the draught by opening and closing gaps in the layer of old bricks on top.

Brick Makers and Cradle Barrow loaded with 'green' bricks at Hedingham Brick and Tile Works towards the end of the last century.

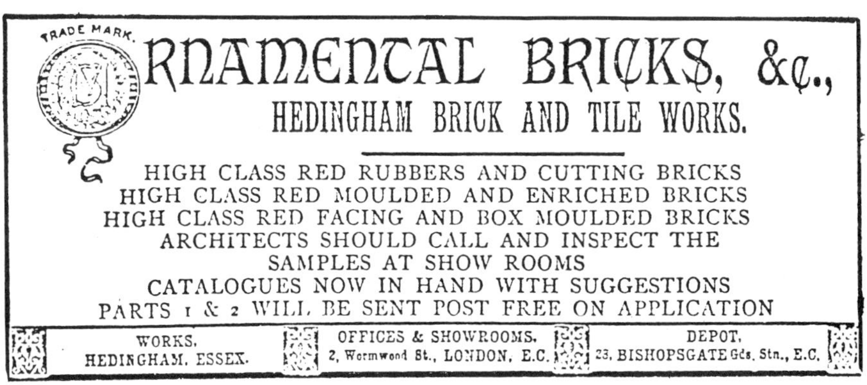

Advertisement dated 1886

Loading bricks onto trucks at the Hedingham Brick and Tile Works siding from the Colne Valley and Halstead Railway in 1897. The man in the bowler hat is Eli Cornish who was then Manager of these Brick Works. John Corder who burnt the bricks is on top of the kiln and one of his sons Edward Corder is standing on the left.

Advertisement of 1892

The Sible Hedingham Red Brick Company Limited showing the three down draught type kilns and two chimneys with the hacks and drying sheds in the centre background. This brickworks was situated at Purlshill, Sible Hedingham and closed in the early 1950's.

The Sible Hedingham Red Brick Company Limited was incorporated in 1919 and its first Directors were Eli Cornish, J.P., (Managing), Harry Tucker Ripper, William Charlton Ripper and Reuben Hunt (of Earls Colne). These brickworks were situated at Purls Hill where the Hedingham Brick Company (latterly under the ownership of Eli Cornish) and the adjacent Highfields brickworks which had previously belonged to Mark Gentry were previously located.

After the formation of the Sible Hedingham Red Brick Company Limited these brickworks became commonly known as "the New Yard" or "Rippers Brickworks" and a siding connected the works with the Colne Valley and Halstead Railway. Although the majority of bricks manufactured here were hand made a brick-making machine was used latterly. In 1954 this was the last of the numerous brickworks which once existed in the Hedinghams to close. It was followed some ten years later with the closure of the Colne Valley Railway.

The Sible Hedingham Red Brick Company Limited showing a kiln being fired by Albert Redgewell. Note the heaps of coal surrounding the kiln and the stack of newly fired bricks in the foreground.

HEDINGHAM BRICKS IN USE

Workman building one of the two bungalows (now 136 and 138 Swan Street) next to the Chemists shop in Swan Street in 1925. The main contractor for building these bungalows was Percy Parr who was a Builder living at Church Street, Castle Hedingham. Left to Right: Albert Martin, Percy Ralph Bareham, Percy James Parr, Stanley Wilding and Harry Steward. Albert Martin and the two carpenters (with saws) worked for Bert Corder a Sible Hedingham builder who sub-contracted them to Percy Parr.

BUILDING PLOTS
FOR SALE.
On Main Roads in Castle and Sible Hedingham.
Frontage to suit Purchasers. Depth 300 feet.

Apply PARR, Builder,
CASTLE HEDINGHAM.

Advertisement of 1925

Hedingham bricks used to build a house on School Hill, Sible Hedingham about 1920. The men are left to right top row: Ben Howe and Alf Steward. Front row: Tom Ward, Herb Brett, Percy Corder, Fred Ruffle and Jack Harrod.

THE CASTLE AND SIBLE HEDINGHAM JOINT FIRE BRIGADE

Although photographed at Castle Hedingham, the firemen are those of the Castle and Sible Hedingham Joint Brigade. Sible Hedingham Parish Council elected five representatives onto the Joint Committee which existed until 1929. Firemen on this photograph include: William Radley (the captain and driver), Nunn Schooling, William Smith, Robert Smith, ? Farrant, Horace W. Alpe, Harry Wright, Tills Kendall and James Earey. The fire engine was a Merryweathers modern manual purchased in 1886 and housed at Castle Hedingham.

When a fire occurred at Rippers Joinery Works at Sible Hedingham on the 4th October, 1914, the brigade did not waste any time waiting for horses, the engine and appliances being run to the scene by hand. They arrived twenty minutes after receiving the call at 4 a.m. and the fire was under control by 9 a.m. Later in the day, Scouts under Scoutmaster Frank Westrop, were on guard at the works ready to quell any further outbreaks. Rippers Limited later had their own manual engine and at another fire on 15th June, 1925 this engine was supported by engines from Halstead and Sudbury as well as the Hedinghams engine.

Another view of the Castle and Sible Hedingham Joint Fire Brigade photographed at Castle Hedingham in front of 'The Three Crowns' Inn which was situated in St. James Street (not to be confused with the 'Crown' Inn in Crown Street). The driver and captain was William Radley who was the landlord of The Three Crowns and later of the Bell Inn. The previous captain was Robert Balls, who was a partner of Balls and Balls, the well known auctioneers, land agents and valuers. The last captain before this volunteer brigade ceased in 1929 was Nunn Schooling.

A FIRE AT RIPPERS WOODWORKS

Firemen damping down after a fire at Rippers Limited in 1914. In the foreground with beard is Tucker Ripper. Percy Corder was with the Sible and Castle Hedingham Joint Fire Brigade fighting the fire and worked many hours without a break.

A view of the damage after the fire. This is one of a number of fires which has occurred at the works over the years.

At another fire in June, 1925 the works fire brigade with its manual engine was joined by the Hedinghams Fire Brigade and also Halstead and Sudbury Brigades. At this fire the main power house and a storage area was destroyed. It took the combined brigades some five hours to get this fire under control and fortunately they were able to prevent it spreading to other buildings.

THE DEVELOPMENT OF RIPPERS LIMITED

Edward Ripper (in bowler hat) with some early workmen at Rippers Joinery Works.

The Hedingham Joinery works of Rippers Limited were established in 1894 when they were situated at the rear of Queen's Street, Castle Hedingham. By 1899, the business had grown to such an extent that more commodious buildings were required and the business moved to its present site on the borders of Castle and Sible Hedingham. By 1909 the three brothers, Tucker, Charlton and Edward Ripper employed about 85 men and twenty years later, by which time a company had been incorporated, about 350 men and staff found employment in the various departments of the works.

When the new site adjacent to the railway station was acquired in 1899 it consisted of about 1½ acres of bare land and a rough shed with a saw pit attached. New workshops and store sheds were immediately built together with four red brick cottages in Station Road for key employees. Further property was purchased adjacent to these new works and more buildings erected. The above photograph shows the construction of an addition in rough weather.

The Joiners' shop which extended to 50 feet by 120 feet. In 1909 there were about 30 skilled men here but in time of pressure there was ample accommodation for over 50 men. The office was on the same floor and beneath this floor were the stores consisting of two floors specially constructed for holding timber. The lower floor was devoted to heavier timber and hard wood such as oak, mahogany and teak whilst the next floor contained lighter timber for making mouldings and panels. In July, 1933 Princess Marie Louise, a cousin of King George V toured the works including the stock yards, saw mill and joinery shops.

An aerial view of the woodworks of Rippers Limited in 1929. On the left is the present A604 road and on the right the former Colne Valley and Halstead Railway with Sible and Castle Hedingham Station and sidings into the woodworks. In the foreground are the former wooden bungalows which were known as "the huts" and in the background houses in Yeldham Road and Station Road built by Rippers Limited for their employees.

Rippers held the idea that the health and contentment of the workers was essential to efficiency and therefore paid attention to the welfare of employees. Two housing schemes were developed one of 50 houses and 13 bungalows and a second of another 50 houses. The company were pioneers of giving paid holidays – a rare luxury!

After the First World War there was a shortage of housing in Sible Hedingham and to help the situation in June, 1920, Rippers Limited presented plans to the former Halstead Rural District Council for the erection of ten wooden bungalows on Brook Farm Hill. Each bungalow contained maximum accommodation of six rooms with a hall running the full length. The occupants initially obtained water from an artesian well at the joinery works until mains water was connected. These bungalows which provided comfortable homes survived until after Rippers Limited were taken over by Bowater when they were demolished to make way for extentions to the factory.

Rippers woodworks, Brook Farm House and "the huts" photographed from Brook Meadow circa 1930's. The Norman Keep of Hedingham Castle is on the horizon (centre) and Rippers water tower on the left. Brook Meadow was developed in 1947/48 as a Council Housing Estate.

Hardwood logs in stick at Rippers works in 1929 when there were over ten acres of sheds and stock grounds for raw material. On the extreme left are two of the wooden bungalows built by the company for employees and their families and behind them the water tower which was a prominent landmark until it was demolished recently. Water was supplied from the works' own artesian well and the tank on top of the tower held 100,000 gallons.

Swan Street about the time of the Second World War with Peter Bareham delivering newspapers from his hand cart. The shop is Douglas Newman's Butchers then owned by his late father Mark Newman. The adjoining house was built by Harry Gooch and the row of houses beyond by Rippers Limited c. 1924/26.

Some more houses built by Rippers Limited in Yeldham Road c. 1926/28. This photograph was taken prior to the Second World War and shows the road before it was straightened and the pavement constructed.

A 'Lock Out' at Rippers joinery works on 1st October, 1907. Men on the photograph include William Drury, Bunny Farrant, Ernie Gepp, Billie Letch, Bill Corder, Ted Corder, Bertie Corder, Sidney Staines, William Letch, Ted Beadle, George Ruffle, Frank Boreham, Lewis Boorer, Jim Springett, Frank Toswell, George Springett and Alfred Underwood.

Men on strike standing on the Green in front of the Grocers and Drapers shop owned by Robert S. Carter at the junction of Swan Street and Alderford Street. Note the Policeman on the left. There appears to be some difference of opinion as to whether these men were from Rippers Limited or from the brickworks of the Hedingham Brick Co. or Rayners brickworks at Maiden Ley. The general opinion is that they were brickmakers and wanted a ½d a thousand extra for making bricks.

Long serving employees at Rippers Limited photographed on the works premises about 1949.
Back row left to right: Alfred Ambrose, Herbert Partridge, Harry Scott, Harry Cansell, Sid Garwood, Tucker Ripper, Ernest Chatten, Stanley Ambrose, Albert Turner and Herbert Schooling.
Front row left to right: Ernest Gepp, Ernie Farrant, George Howard, Lewis Boorer, Frank Westrop, Edward Beadle, Albert Amey, Alec Yerbury, William Beadle.

THE COLNE VALLEY AND HALSTEAD RAILWAY THROUGH HEDINGHAM

Sible and Castle Hedingham Railway Station upon the occasion of the Coronation of King Edward VII in 1902. The Railway Station was built in 1861 and was rebuilt at the Colne Valley Railway Preservation site, Yeldham Road, Castle Hedingham during the 1970's.

The first verse of a poem about the opening of the railway refers to Hedingham Station as follows:–

"In the year eighteen hundred and sixty-one,
The Colne Valley Railway so long begun,
At Hedingham came to a great termination,
Complete with Goods Shed and neat little Station."

For the opening, the bridge at Alderford Hill, Sible Hedingham was decorated, chiefly at the expense of Charles Hilton, who also arranged for the band of the 12th Essex Rifles to play. An aggregate of 1,700 passengers were conveyed on the first day and the trains so crowded that cattle trucks were used as well as carriages. The last up train had to return to Hedingham for 200 passengers who were unable to return by the earlier fixed trains.

Coal being unloaded from trucks on a siding of the Colne Valley and Halstead Railway near Sible Hedingham Station. In the background is a view of Rippers joinery works prior to the First World War.

A busy scene outside Sible and Castle Hedingham Railway Station (centre). On the right is Rippers joinery works and on the left the "Station Malting" which had been owned since 1908 by Thomas Bradridge and Edward Ruggles-Brise (later Col. Sir Edward Ruggles-Brise, Bt., M.C., T.D., D.L., J.P., M.P.,) who traded as Thomas Bradridge & Co., Maltsters, Corn, Seed and Coal Merchants. These maltings were previously owned by Vero Taylor when they were known as the "Halfway House Maltings". In 1926 the Maltings were sold by Thomas Bradridge & Co., to Rippers Limited and later used as part of their joinery works.

The inscription on the original photograph was "Mass Meeting, Sible Hedingham". It is thought that it was taken in 1914 when large meetings were held in the Railway Station Yard to recruit men to serve in the First World War. These meetings were held on 6th September and 18th October, 1914 and were both well attended.

An excursion train arriving at Hedingham Station from Haverhill probably during the early 1900's. The length of the train indicates that crowds were expected and judging by the large number of people waiting on the platform the Colne Valley and Halstead Railway were not disappointed.

This locomotive of the old Colne Valley and Halstead Railway was named "Hedingham" and was obviously decorated for a public occasion such as a Jubilee or Coronation. For the railway enthusiast "Hedingham" was a 2–4–2 side tank locomotive and was used on the line from 1894 to 1923. "Hedingham" which was given the number "4" was built in 1894, rebuilt in 1902 and ceased being used in 1923 when the London North Eastern Railway took over the Colne Valley and Halstead Railway.

MORE PUBLIC TRANSPORT AND HAULAGE

Mark John Glover Gentry, son of Mark Gentry the well known Sible Hedingham Master Brick-maker, with a car for public hire. Mark Gentry, junior, started a motor and engineering works in about 1904 at his fathers brickworks in Wethersfield Road. He later established the garage in Swan Street (opposite Alexandra Road) where this photograph was taken.

He had cars for hire and sold petrol, oil and all accessories. In August, 1907 he purchased a motor bus which ran to Braintree, Sudbury and Haverhill on the respective market days of those towns. He sold all makes of ploughshares and fittings and carried out engineering and haulage work. He held the agency for the Eros Ford Tractor Attachment which converted any Ford motor car into a Farm Tractor for ploughing (2 furrows) or haulage work up to 10 tons. In 1917 he sold his garage and tractor business and died the following year.

Aubrey Letch was one of the earliest bus proprietors in the area. He is standing near the front of his first vehicle photographed at High Street Green. It was a First World War ambulance which Aubrey Letch converted into a 14 seater bus with the help of friends in 1919. Also included in this photograph are Aubrey Letch's parents and on the left is Samuel Dyson.

Frederick George Bishop of Alderford Mill carried on a road haulage business as well as being a miller and corn merchant. George Bishop, as he was known, owned a number of steam engines for haulage (and threshing) including this Wallis and Stevens 4¼ ton steam tractor seen hauling its load. These tractors were used for haulage to as far afield as London and Kent and with a speed limit of 5 m.p.h. these journeys took many hours. (Photograph courtesy of R.L.S. collection).

THE FIRST AND SECOND WORLD WARS

A large number of Sible Hedingham men and women served their King and Country during both World Wars many of whom made the supreme sacrifice.

The First World War

On the outbreak of the First World War in August, 1914 there were a few men from the village already serving in the forces as regulars. In addition a number of men volunteered their services. The first seven men to volunteer from Sible Hedingham in August, 1914 were:–

William Dan Corder	Essex Regiment
Alfred Charles Drury	Essex Regiment
Frederick Heavingham	Essex Regiment
Fred Springett	Essex Regiment
Herbert W. Ward	Royal Garrison Artillery
Thomas Ward	Royal Garrison Artillery
William Jack Wiseman	Essex Regiment

By September, 1914 there were a total of 57 men serving, including the regulars, increasing to 72 in February, 1915. When Herbert White, a Blacksmith of Swan Street enlisted as a farrier in the Army Service Corps in September, 1915 he made the number of Sible Hedingham men serving up to 100. Although over military age he was anxious to do "his bit" and volunteered when the need for farriers in cavalry depots was so great. He was drafted to Greece and later to Egypt where he served for two years until his death.

The first three Sible Hedingham men to be killed in 1914 were:–

Pte. John Brett	2nd Batt. Essex Regiment
Pte. Harry Rayner	1st Batt. Bedfordshire Regiment
Pte. Roger Springett	2nd Batt. Suffolk Regiment

The first Sible Hedingham man to be taken a prisoner of war was Pte. Percy Parr of the Suffolk Regiment whose home was at Alexandra Road. He left England for France on 13th August and took part in the engagement at Mons on 23rd August, 1914. He went into action against the enemy at Le Cateau where he was captured on 26th August. After eighteen months at a prisoner of war camp at Doeberitz he worked for three years in a coal mine for 12 hours a day, seven days a week. After four and a half years captivity he returned to Hedingham in January, 1919 and later commenced his own building business operating from Castle Hedingham.

The Sible Hedingham Rifle Club began in May, 1915 and used a meadow at the rear of the Swan Inn. This provided potential servicemen with the opportunity to practice shooting at targets and familiarize themselves with guns. As the war progressed recruiting became more intense and the former Assembly Rooms in Swan Street were used for this purpose.

On 25th January, 1916 the first batch of recruits from Sible Hedingham and surrounding villages to be called up under Lord Derby's scheme left by train from Sible and Castle Hedingham station. This calling up affected farmers and other employers many of whom were already working with depleted staffs. By April, 1916 a Mrs. J. Ridgewell, two of whose sons were serving in the army, started work on a farm belonging to Sidney Everton Halls of Blois Hall. A Halstead Gazette reporter found her sitting on a drill and driving the horses. The report stated that she was "the first patriotic woman to work the land in this part of the country".

A few of the lady employees at Rippers Limited during the First World War who made wooden parts for aeroplanes. From the left: Ethel Underwood (later Ethel Redgewell), May Corder, Dolly Banks (later Dolly Smith), unknown and Elsie Harper. The "dispersal" of the lady aircraft workers at Rippers took place in March, 1919.

By 1917 women were undertaking all kinds of work owing to so many men having enlisted. At Sible Hedingham a number of women were trained as bell ringers under the supervision of Lewis Wiseman which was the first instance of women undertaking bell ringing in North Essex.

By the end of the First World War over 320 Sible Hedingham men had served their King and Country of whom 52 lost their lives.

The following is a list of those who served. The letters against some names indicate:–

k = killed
w = wounded
d = died
p = prisoner
g = gassed

Ashley Adkins, Labour Company, Army Service Corps
Mark Edwin Aldridge, Labour Corps/Suffolk Regiment
Lieut. E. Allingham, Royal Air Force
(w) Pte. Ernest Albert Alliston, 11th Batt. Essex Regiment
(d) Pte. Louis Alliston, 5th Batt. Essex Regiment
Samuel Alliston, Royal Garrison Artillery
L/Cpl. H. Ambrose, 10th Batt. Essex Regiment
Frank Bacon, Labour Coy/Essex Regiment
Harry Bacon, Essex Regiment
A.E. Bareham, 36th Batt. Royal Fusiliers
M.T.W. Bareham, (or Bearham) Royal Flying Corps
Pte. Percy William Bareham, 11th Batt. Essex Regt./Beds & Herts Regt.
S.E. Bareham, Rifle Brigade
(w) Bombardier William K. Bareham, Royal Garrison Artillery
(k) Pte. Charles Thomas Beaney, 2nd Batt. Essex Regiment
1st A/M, J.W. Bearman, Royal Air Force
J.F. Bell, Royal Army Medical Corps
Cpl. E. Berry, Royal Army Medical Corps
(w) Lieut. Adrian Bing, 1st Middlesex Regiment
(k) Pte. Alfred Boreham, 1/5th Essex Regiment
(w) & (p) Pte. A. Ernest Boreham, 1/5th Essex Regiment
(k) Pte. Benjamin Boreham, 3/5th Essex Regiment
(k) Pte. Charles Humphrey Boreham, 7th Middlesex Regiment
(k) Pte. Dollar Signor Boreham, Northamptonshire Regt./Essex Regt.
(g) Pte. Edie Boreham, Essex Regiment
(d) Pte. Ernest J. Boreham, 1st Batt. Essex Regiment
(w) & (g) Frank Boreham, Essex Regiment
George O. Boreham, Labour Coy/6th Batt. Essex Regiment
(k) Pte. Harry Boreham, 2nd Essex Regiment
(k) Pte. Harry Robert Boreham, 2nd Batt. Essex Regiment
(k) Pte. H. Boreham, Essex Regiment
H. Boreham, Royal Air Force
James Vero Boreham, Essex Regiment/5th Batt. Northampton Regt.
J.W. Boreham, Labour Corps
Percy M. Boreham, Royal Fusiliers/6th Batt. Essex Regiment
R. Boreham, Essex Regiment
W. Boreham, Bedfordshire & Hertfordshire Regiment

(d) Pte. Harry Herbert Boulton, Royal West Kent Regt./Middlesex Regt.
(w) Lieut. John Sidey Braine, 2nd Duke of Wellingtons Regiment
Lieut. W.T. Coker Braine, West Riding Regiment
(p) Pte. Herbert Brett, 14th Batt. Essex Regiment/4th Batt. Middlesex Regt.
(k) Pte. John Brett, 2nd Batt. Essex Regiment
L/Cpl. Maurice Brett, Machine Gun Corps
Walter Brett, Army Service Corps
G. Britton, Royal Field Artillery
Herbert George John Britton, Royal Army Medical Corps
Ernest William Broyd, Royal Garrison Artillery
(k) Rifleman, William George Bruty, Kings Royal Rifles
F.J. Bull, Middlesex Regiment
1st Class P.O Sidney Bull, H.M.S. Halcyon, Royal Navy
Harry Vernon Bull, Suffolk Regiment (Suffolk Cyclists)
G. Burden, Royal Field Artillery
Sidney E. Butcher, Royal Garrison Artillery
(k) Pte. Ernest G. Byford, 9th Batt. Essex Regiment
(k) Pte. E. Byford, 59th Canadians
Pte. Walter Byford, 3rd Batt. Essex Regiment
(p) & (g) Chief Gunner C.J. Byrne, H.M.S. Teviot and H.M.S. India, Royal Navy
3rd A/M Albert Carter, Royal Air Force
Frederick Carter, Royal Flying Corps
(k) Pte. Frederick George Chapman, M.M., 5th Northamptonshire Regt.
Bdr. H. Chapman, Royal Field Artillery
(w) Pte. Arthur Chinnery, Essex Regiment/Army Service Corps
(w) Sgt. Albert Choat, Royal Field Artillery
(w) Fred Clark, Essex Regiment/Lincolnshire Regiment
1st Echelon, V.A. Clark, Army Veterinary Corps
(w) Sgt. John ("Jack") William Coates, Essex Regiment
Edward Cock, The Buffs
Lieut. W. Coleman, Ontario Canadian Scottish Contingent
M. Cook, Essex Regiment
Walter Herbert Cook, Army Service Corps
(w) Pte. Fred Corder, 12th Batt. Essex Regiment/Machine Gun Corps/ Royal Fusiliers and Royal West Kent (Queens Own) Regiment
Pte. Herbert Charles Corder, Army Service Corps
(w) Rflm. John Corder, Kings Royal Rifles
(w) Rflm. Percy James Corder, 9th Rifle Brigade, Kings Royal Rifles
(w) Rflm. Walter Edward Corder, Kings Royal Rifles/Labour Corps
(w) Spr. William Dan Corder, Essex Regiment/Royal Engineers
(g) & (w) Captain Fred Cornish, Essex Yeomanry, The Inns of Court Officers Training Corps, Royal Flying Corps (later R.A.F.), 1st East Yorkshire Regiment
(w) Archibald Frederick Cox, 1/7th Middlesex Regiment
William Cox, Army Service Corps
(w) C. Cross, Leicester Regiment/1st Lancaster Regiment

(w) D. Cross, 1st Leicester Regiment
E. Cross, 12th Essex Regiment/Lancaster Regiment
Band-boy Edmund Cross, Essex Regiment/1st Lancaster Regiment
(w) J. Cross, 13th Field Ambulance, Royal Army Medical Corps
(p) Pte. William Cross, Wiltshire Regiment/Army Remount Depot
Spr. Rufus Cudmore, Royal Engineers
Able Seaman Bert Cutter, H.M.S. Hydria, Royal Navy
(w) Charles Cutter, 2nd Batt. Essex Regiment/Army Service Corps
Percy Albert Cutter, Essex Regiment/Bedfordshire Regiment
(w) Pte. William Cutter, Essex Regiment
(k) Pte. Albert John Daines, 5th Connaught Rangers
H. Daines, 51st Leicesters
(k) Pte. Harry Bertie Daines, Kings Own Royal Lancaster Regiment
(w) Pte. Joseph C. Daines, Essex Regiment/Navy/L.D. Labour Centre
(w) Pte. Sidney Daines, Machine Gun Corps
(k) Pte. William Ernest Daines, 11th Batt. Essex Regiment
(k) Pte. George Ralph Dowsett, Royal West Surrey
(p) Pte. Alfred Charles Drury, Essex Regiment/Motor Transport, Army Service Corps
(k) L/Cpl. Fred Drury, D.C.M., 5th Batt. Northamptonshire Regiment
F.A. Drury, Rifle Brigade
(w) Pte. George Drury, Northampton Regiment
(w) Rifleman A.J. Earey, 17th Kings Royal Rifle Corps
Spr. E. Earey, Royal Engineers
(d) Pte. R. Earey, Essex Regiment
(d) Pte. Walter Henry Earey, 9th Batt. Essex Regiment
(k) Cpl. Alan Sidney Elsdon, 1st East Surrey Regiment
(w) George Thomas Elsdon, Royal Flying Corps
Harry Claude Elsdon, Northamptonshire Regiment
L. Elsdon, East Surrey Regiment
(k) Pte. Albert C. Everitt, 8th Beds & Herts Regiment
Ernest I. Everitt, 1st Bedfords/8th Batt. Northamptonshire Regt.
(k) Pte. Frederick George Everitt, 12th Essex Regt./Middlesex Regt.
Harry Everitt
(p) Thomas Edward Everitt, Wiltshire Regiment
(w) William Everitt, West Yorkshire Regiment
W. Everitt, Hampshire Regiment
William Farrant, Royal Marine Light Infantry
Arthur Charles Finch, Royal Garrison Artillery
Charles Finch, Machine Gun Corps
(k) Pte. John ("Jack") Finch, 17th Batt. Royal Fusiliers
John Finch, Labour Corps
C. Fletcher, Kings Light Horse
Sidney Fletcher, Queens Royal West Surrey Regiment
Spr. Walter Fletcher, Royal Engineers
William Fletcher, Labour Corps/Middlesex Regiment

W. Fletcher, Royal Marines
Pte. Hubert Gibson, Motor Transport, Army Service Corps
B. Giles, Royal Navy
(w) Pte. Harold Goode, Middlesex Regiment
(k) Pte. William J. Gooderham, 17th Batt. Royal Fusiliers
B. Hale, Royal Navy
(w) Pte. Bernard George Hale, M.M., East Kent Regiment, (Buffs)
Trooper Horace Scott Hale, Royal Field Artillery/Essex Yeomanry
J. Hale, Royal Navy
R. Hale, Royal Navy
T. Hale, Royal Navy
B. Halls, Suffolk Regiment/Labour Corps
(w) & (p) Pte. Leonard Handscombe, Essex Regiment/Machine Gun Corps
C. Harbour, Royal Field Artillery
(w) Rflm. E.W. Harding, Rifle Brigade
F. Harding, Army Veterinary Corps
(w) F. Harding, Rifle Brigade/Labour Corps
H. Harding, Labour Corps
Cpl. Albert F. Hardy, Army Veterinary Corps
Victor A. Hardy, Army Veterinary Corps
Stanley Harper, 3rd Batt. Norfolk Regiment/Royal Fusiliers
(k) Pte. Harry Harrington, 7th Batt. Essex Regt./17th Batt. Middlesex Regt.
(k) Pte. William Harrington, 7th Batt. Essex Regiment/Royal Fusiliers
C. Harrod, Royal Flying Corps
Charles Harrod, H.M.S. President II, Royal Navy
Spr. Charles J. Harrod, Royal Engineers
William J. Harrod, 1/6th Essex Regiment
Frederick Heavingham, Essex Regiment
(w) Percy Heavingham, Essex Regiment
R. Heavingham, Royal West Surrey
(w) Cpl. Charles Hickford, Royal Field Artillery
G.A. Horsley, Suffolk Regiment
Able Seaman Ben Howe, H.M.S. Havelock, Royal Navy
D. Jarrad, Royal Horse Artillery
Captain Robert Spencer Johnstone, O.B.E.
(k) Rflm. Albert Kendall, Kings Royal Rifles
A. Kendall, Army Service Corps
Bertie William Kendall, Essex Yeomanry/Royal Garrison Artillery
F. Kendall, Royal Naval Air Service
(w) Sgt. Fred W. Kendall, Royal West Kent Regiment/Middlesex Regiment
George Kendall, 9th Batt. Essex Regiment
Harry Kendall, Labour Coy
Harold Stanley Kendall, Royal Field Artillery
R. Kendall, Royal Navy
(p) Sidney Kendall, H.M.S. President, Royal Navy
Seaman S.A. Kendall, Royal Marines

(k) Pte. William Kendall, Royal Sussex Regiment
W. Kendall, 5th Royal Inniskilling Fusiliers
(k) Pte. Walter Kendall, 10th Batt. Beds & Herts Regiment
W.G. Kendall, Labour Corps
Reginald Robert Kiddy, Essex Yeomanry
B. King, Essex Regiment
Percy William King, Essex Regiment
A.S. Lavender, Essex Yeomanry
Lieut. J.A. Lawson, South African Infantry
Aubrey Letch, Motor Transport, Army Service Corps
(w) Rflm. Ernest Letch, Kings Royal Rifles
(k) Pte. Ernest William Letch, 3rd London/Kings Royal Rifles
(d) Pte. Frank Letch, 11th Essex Regiment
George Walter Letch, Army Service Corps
H. Letch, Essex Regiment
(w) Walter Letch, Labour Corps, Kings Royal Rifles, 1/19th London Regt.
3rd A.M., A.C. Lewsey, Royal Air Force
Spr. E. Lewsey, Royal Engineers
(k) Pte. George C. Linsell, 8th Batt. Beds & Herts Regiment
Ernest Lock, Labour Corps/Kings Royal Rifles
(g) & (w) Signaller Fred Lock, 11th Batt. Essex Regiment
L/Cpl. William George Lodge, Middlesex Regiment, Military Police
H.H. Lorkin, Middlesex Regiment
David (Joe) Mansfield, Army Service Corps
William George Mansfield, Northamptonshire Regiment
(k) Pte. Arthur S. Martin, 25th Canadian Regiment
(w) L/Cpl. E.G. Martin, 2nd Batt. Essex Regiment
Sgt. Cecil Geoffrey Mayn, Army Ordnance
(k) Pte. Edward Mead, Essex Territorials/Essex Regiment/Royal Sussex
(p) Ernest Herbert Mead, 7th Batt. Essex Regiment/East Kents (Buffs)/ East Surrey Regiment
Lieut. Frederick John Mead, Cavalry (later Col. F.J. Mead, C.B.E.) The Royal North West Mounted Police
Sgt. George William Mead, M.M., Royal Garrison Artillery
William Frederick Meadowcroft, Royal Army Medical Corps
Fred Golden Metson, Royal Flying Corps/Royal Air Force
Sidney Thomas Metson, Army Service Corps
A.E. Mitchell, Essex Yeomanry
L. Mitchell, Essex Yeomanry
Frederick Monk, Royal Garrison Artillery
B.C. Mortimer, Army Service Corps
I. Murray, H.M.S. Cyclops, Royal Navy
Harry North, Royal Engineers/Essex Regiment/Royal Navy
Sgt. J.V. Owens, 2nd Batt., Cameronians, Scottish Rifles
Arthur Pannell, Royal Navy
(k) Gunner Fred Pannell, D.C.M., Royal Garrison Artillery

(w) Rflm. Hubert Pannell, Kings Royal Rifles
(p) Pte, Percy James Parr, Suffolk Regiment
(k) Pte. Ernest Sidney Partridge, 13th Batt. Royal Sussex Regiment
Lieut. A. Perkins, East Surrey Regiment
(k) Pte. Bert Pettitt, 1st Batt. Suffolk Regiment
Pte. E. Pettitt, 9th Batt. Essex Regiment
L/Cpl. J. Pettitt, Machine Gun Corps/Kings Royal Rifles
Edward Pilgrim, Royal Navy
P. Pilgrim, Royal Navy
John Wilkin Porkess, Motor Transport Company
(k) Sapper Edgar Rayner, Royal Engineers
(k) Pte. Harry Rayner, Bedfordshire & Hertfordshire Regiment
(w) & (g) Sgt. Percy Ronald Rayner, Kings Royal Rifles
Captain William Wright Raynham, D.C.M., Northumberland Fusiliers
Harry Raymond, Essex Regiment/Labour Corps/Beds & Herts Regiment
(k) Rflm. Arthur Redgewell, 18th Kings Royal Rifles
A. Redgewell, Army Service Corps
Cpl. A. Redgewell
(w) Sgt. Ernest Redgewell, Royal Air Force
(w) Sgt. Ernest William Redgewell, 1st Batt. Essex Regiment/Royal Flying Corps
A/M Fred Redgewell, Royal Air Force
G. Redgewell, 5th Connaught Rangers
(w) James Redgewell, King Royal Rifles
A. Ridgewell, Army Service Corps
(k) Cpl. Arthur Frederick Ridgewell, M.S.M., 5th Essex Regiment
George E. Ridgewell, 2nd Batt. Essex Regiment/Kings Royal Rifles
(d) Pte. John Charles Ridgewell, Northants Regiment/Kings Royal Rifles
Sgt. Major F. Robinson, Royal Field Artillery
Spr. Charles A. Robson, 31st Signalling Company Royal Engineers
L/Cpl. Percy S. Robson, 25th Signalling Company Royal Engineers
(w) Driver Albert Ruffle, Royal Field Artillery
(k) Pte. Alfred E. Ruffle, 9th Batt. Essex Regiment
Fred Ruffle, Royal Naval Air Service
Spr. F. Ruffle, Royal Engineers
Spr. Francis George Ruffle, Royal Engineers
(k) Pte. F.M.? or M.F.? Ruffle, Essex Regiment
L. Ruffle, Essex Regiment
S. Ruffle, The Queen's Royal West Surrey's
Thomas Ruffle, Army Ordnance Corps
Walter William Ruffle, Army Ordnance Corps
W.F. Ruffle, Labour Corps
Harry Ruggles, 10th Batt. Essex Regiment
I. Ruggles, Royal Garrison Artillery
H.G. Rulton, 5th Batt. Essex Regiment
Spr. H.A. Sandford, Royal Canadian Engineers

Sgt. V.A. Sandford, M.T. Canadian Army Service Corps
Spr. H. Schooling, Royal Engineers
(w) Pte. O.R. Simpson, Labour Corps, 7th Beds & Herts Regiment
(w) A.G. Smith, Royal Engineers
C.P. Smith, Machine Gun Corps
Cornelius Walter Smith, R.A.M.C./Kings Royal Rifles/Royal Engineers
(w) Pte. Fred Smith, 3rd Scottish Borderers
George Edward Smith, Cameronians
Humphrey Sidney Smith, Labour Corps, Machine Gun Corps/Essex Regiment
Rflm. J. Smith, Kings Royal Rifles
W.C. Smith, S & C.S., Royal Engineers
Col. Richard Sparrow, C.M.G., D.S.O., F.R.G.S., F.Z.S., M.B.O.U., J.P., 7th Dragoon Guards
(d) Driver Bertram Springett, Royal Field Artillery
Pioneer C. Springett, 11th Batt. Essex Regiment
E.J. Springett, M.T., A.S.C.
Fred Springett, Essex Regiment
(w) George Springett, 3rd Welsh
(k) Pte. Roger Springett, 2nd Batt. Suffolk Regiment
Stanley Springett, Royal Flying Corps
Edgar Joseph Spurgeon, Motor Transport, Army Service Corps
E.G. Staines, H.M.S. Canterbury, Royal Navy
W.H. Staines, Essex Regiment
Alfred Basil Steward, Royal Navy
(w) Pte. Bert Steward, 11th Batt. Essex Regiment/Suffolk Regiment
C. Steward, Signal Company, Royal Engineers
C. Alfred Steward, Army Service Corps
F. Steward, Essex Regiment
F. Steward, Royal Marines
(k) Pte. Francis Thomas Steward, 11th Royal Fusiliers
A.A. Taylor, Essex Regiment
David Taylor, Army Service Corps
Sgt. Frederick Taylor, Motor Transport, Army Service Corps
Co.-Qr. Master-Sergt. William J. Taylor, Army Service Corps
Driver Frank Tokley, Royal Horse Artillery
Sgt. John Tokley, Cambridgeshire Regiment
(k) Pte. Thomas Robert Tokley, Royal Army Medical Corps
(w) Lieut. Henry Eric Russell Twamley, Sherwood Foresters/Royal Flying Corps
A.A. Tyler, 9th Batt. Essex Regiment
Rflm. Norman G. Vagg, Kings Royal Rifles
(k) Pte. Alfred J. Vale, 2/5th Essex Regiment/9th London Regiment
2nd-Lieut. Thomas Mumford Vale, Essex Regiment/Northumberland Fusiliers
G. Walker, Royal Garrison Artillery

W. Walker, Royal Fusiliers
William Thomas Walker, Labour Coy
Archibald William B. Wapling, Queen Victoria Rifles
Leonard George B. Wapling, Royal Defence Corps/London Irish
(k) S.R.B. Wapling, London Scottish
Harry Ward, Army Ordnance Corps
Herbert W. Ward, Royal Garrison Artillery
(g) Cpl. Leonard Alfred Ward, Royal Field Artillery
(w) Pte. Simeon Ward, Coldstream Guards
Thomas Ward, Royal Garrison Artillery
(w) William Ward, Essex Regiment
William Ward, 5th Batt. Essex Regiment
L/Cpl. Philip Warren, Essex Yeomanry
(k) Pte. Albert V. Watson, Beds & Herts Regiment/Northumberland Regiment/Northants Regiment
(k) Pte. Frederick J. Watson, 3rd Batt. Grenadier Guards
(d) Pte. Farrier Herbert ('Bert') White, Royal Army Service Corps
Sgt. T. Whitehead, D.C.M., M.M., Royal Garrison Artillery
E. Wilding, Motor Transport, Army Service Corps
Frank Wilding, Army Service Corps
(w) Pte. Frederick Wilding, 9th Batt. Essex Regiment
G.H. Wilding, Army Service Corps
Pte. William Willett, Essex Regiment/Royal Fusiliers
Walter Edward Willsher, Duke of Cornwalls Light Infanty
A. Wiseman, Royal Fusiliers
(k) Pte. Freddie Maurice Wiseman, 11th Queens Royal West Surrey Regt.
(w) Herbert Frederick Wiseman, Essex Regt./Northamptonshire Regt.
(p) L/Cpl. Harry Wiseman, Kings Royal Rifles
L/Cpl. H. Wiseman, Army Service Corps
Maurice Wiseman, 2/5th Middlesex Regiment
R. Wiseman, Middlesex Regiment
W.G. Wiseman, Royal Garrison Artillery
William Jack Wiseman, Essex Regiment
Arthur Yeldham, 12th Batt. Essex Regiment
(k) Pte. A.G. Yeldham, 5th Connaught Rangers

Nurse Katherine Elizabeth Deeks, C.C. Station, B.E.F. France
Nurse Eileen Twamley, Red Cross and Friends Ambulance Unit, V.A.D. France

Whilst every effort has been made to ensure that the above list is complete and accurate the reader must appreciate that it was common particularly in the First World War for men to be transferred from one regiment to another. Therefore other records may reveal varying particulars. For example Thomas Vale served in the Essex Regiment, the Northumberland Fusiliers and the Royal Flying Corps whilst Fred Cornish served in the Essex Yeomanry, The Inns of Court, Officers Training Corps and the Royal Flying Corps later the Royal Air Force. One Sible Hedingham man served in no less than four regiments namely Fred Corder who enlisted into the 12th Essex Regiment, was transferred to the Machine Gun Corps, the Royal Fusiliers and latterly the Royal West Kent (Queens Own).

In addition to those on active service there were a number of men in 'B Reserves' including the following:–

Fred G. Amey
William Ashley
Herbert G. Audus
Percy J. Barker
William Beadle
George W. Bickers
Fred C. Boreham
Sidney Boreham
George H. Brett
Walter Britton
George Burder
William E.C. Calver
Fred Cooper
Bertie William Corder
Edward John Corder
Harry Corder
Arthur G. Drury
Albert George Elsdon
Albert C. Everitt
Robert Albert E. Foster
Fred Gatward
Ernest E. Gepp
John Cecil Goodchild
Sidney S. Hale
Sidney E. Halls
Arthur R. Handscombe
George Harper
Robert Harper
George A. Howard
Hector S. Hunwick
George W. Hurrell
George William Jarvis
E.J. Kiddy
Ernest King
Fred King
George W. Letch
Herbert Lock
Joseph C. Mead
Arthur S. Metson
Charles S. Metson
Mark Newman
Herbert Partridge
Herbert Pilgrim
Francis R. Potter
Alfred Scott
Harry W. Scott
George E. Smith
Samuel Smith
Robert Stanhope
Jethro Stimson
William Theobald
Charles Wheeler
A.A. Wiseman

The above names are compiled from a list made in 1916 and it is therefore highly probable that other men were later in B. Reserves. In the original list were the names of numerous men who later went on active service who have been deleted from the above B Reserve list and included on the active service list.

There were several other men willing to serve King and Country but were rejected on medical grounds including the following:–

William Ablitt	Percy H. Howard
Bertie A. Bareham	Edgar Kendall
E. Bayley	Harry Kendall
Sidney F. Bearman	Herbert Mead
Harry Cansell	Arthur E. Parr
W. Cook	Bernard Pettitt
Robert Drury	Frederick Ruffle
Samuel Earey	William Ruffle
Ernest Everitt	George Springett
Harry Everitt	Alfred J. Spurgeon
Mark Gentry	Fred Taylor
Sidney G. Harrington	Fred H. Wash
Albert F. Hardy	Percy H. Wiseman
Victor A. Hardy	Frank Woodcock
Hector Howard	

There were numerous examples of brothers serving and from two Sible Hedingham families no less than six brothers from each family were serving at the same time. One was the Boreham family of Cobbs Fenn only four of whom returned home. Charles Humphrey Boreham of the 7th Middlesex Regiment died of wounds on the 8th May, 1917 and Dollar Boreham of the Northamptonshire Regiment was killed in action early the same year. A contemporary report stated that this family was "doing its bit".

The six sons of David Cross of Sible Hedingham all served in the army and by May 1916 three of them had been wounded. In two other families three sons were taken and in four families two sons.

It is not surprising that with so many men on active service some of them were awarded honours:–

Private Frederick George Chapman, M.M., Northamptonshire Regiment

George Chapman lived at High House and was awarded the Military Medal for bringing in wounded under fire during an engagement in France in 1916.

Lance Corporal Fred Drury, D.C.M., 5th Northamptonshire Regiment

Fred Drury lived at Alderford Street being a son of Henry Drury and was awarded the Distinguished Conduct Medal during the engagement at Loos in September, 1915. The Northamptons were one of the battalions which formed the British attacking force and Drury acted as one of the bombing party. The British Force was exposed to heavy fire from big guns, machine guns and rifles and the

Northamptons suffered rather severely. Drury's good work in the bombing party had been noticed and when things got a little quieter he left the trenches and went out into the open to try and bring in some of the wounded. As soon as the Germans saw him they opened fire with machine guns and rifles, but despite the terrible danger, Drury was not hit and succeeded in bringing back three men, a sergeant and two privates, making three journeys under heavy fire. For those acts of heroism he was awarded the D.C.M. and was also promoted to the rank of Lance Corporal. He was killed on 1st June, 1917 in France.

Private Bernard G. Hale, M.M., East Kent Regiment (Buffs)

Bernard Hale lived at Station Cottages, Sible Hedingham and was awarded the Military Medal for gallantry displayed in action in France in October, 1918. The following is the official version of the brave act which won the medal:–

> "For conspicuous gallantry and devotion to duty in that at Coulin on 8th October, 1918 he volunteered to go out on patrol with two other men to try and spot a machine gun post which was causing many casualties; both his companions were wounded by machine gun fire. He first brought back one into safety and then returned for the other, whom he also got into safety; he then volunteered to guide an officer and party by a covered way which he had found to surround the post, which he did enabling the officer to capture the post, thus saving many lives. He went out on patrol again the following night but was unfortunately wounded."

As a result of these wounds it was found necessary to amputate one leg and the other was also badly injured.

Captain Robert Spencer Johnstone, O.B.E

Robert Johnstone formerly lived at Bakers, Sible Hedingham and was awarded the Officer of the British Empire Medal in 1920 for distinction during five years service to the country during the First World War. It is understood that he invented a bomb. He was also made a Fellow of the Geographical Society and a member of Trinity House.

Sergeant George William Mead, M.M., Royal Garrison Artillery

George Mead lived at Paste House, (formerly Pest House) Sible Hedingham and was awarded the Military Medal whilst a Corporal in 1916 for good work in the field. He had served in France since 1914 being one of the original British Expeditionary Force and was in the thickest of the heavy fighting. He died at Cambridge Avenue, Sible Hedingham in March, 1944.

His brother was Deputy Commissioner Colonel Frederick John Mead, C.B.E., of the Royal Canadian Mounted Police

Fred Mead was born in Sible Hedingham and was employed by Rippers woodworks for a short time after leaving school. At the age of 16 he left England for Canada and in 1910 joined the R.C.M.P. He served with the rank of Lieutenant in France and Belgium in the First World War with the Royal North West Mounted Police contingent and during this time visited Hedingham. Although promotions were hard earned, he climbed the ladder quickly and in 1944 was made Deputy Commissioner, the second highest rank in the R.C.M.P. This was the highest rank in the Force to which, one, not born in Canada could rise. In 1946 he was awarded the C.B.E. His retirement in 1948 was marked with high tributes for his work and devotion to duty. In 1914, he had been commended for his outstanding efforts and zeal in the Hillcrest Coal Mine disaster in Alberta. In 1926 he made an arduous one thousand mile dog sled patrol to Trout Lake in Northern Ontario upon an investigation. After the attack on Pearl Harbour in 1941 he was one of three R.C.M.P. representatives on the British Columbia Security Commission to remove all Japanese residents from protected areas on Canada's Pacific coast. He died at his home in Vancouver, Canada on 9th September, 1961 aged 72 years and was buried with full Military Honours.

As a native of Sible Hedingham, he probably became one of its most distinguished sons this century.

Gunner Fred Pannell, D.C.M., Royal Garrison Artillery

Fred Pannell lived at High Street Green and was awarded the Distinguished Conduct Medal in 1917 for gallantry on the battlefield. At the outbreak of war he was serving in India and was killed whilst serving with General Townsend's Forces at Kut-el-Amarah against the Turks.

Captain William Wright Raynham, D.C.M., Northumberland Fusiliers

William Raynham was an old soldier who had taken part in the South African and Egyptian campaigns. He lived in Church Street, where he was a Baker, until he rejoined the Northumberland Fusiliers in the First World War. He was given a commission in December, 1915 and was the recipient of a Distinguished Conduct Medal. After the war he was employed by Rippers Limited and lived at Crosspath near the works. He died at Witham on 31st January, 1953 aged 75 years.

William Raynham photographed after the Boer War wearing his Egyptian and South African campaign medals.

Corporal Arthur Frederick Ridgewell, M.S.M., 5th Essex Regiment

Arthur Frederick Ridgewell lived at Blois End and was awarded the Meritorious Service Medal by the British Military Authorities. He also received the Belgian Decoration Militaire for bravery displayed. He was mentioned in despatches by Sir Douglas Haig and gave his life for his country whilst serving in France on 12th September, 1918.

Colonel Richard Sparrow, C.M.G., D.S.O., F.R.G.S., F.Z.S., M.B.O.U., J.P., (1871–1953) 7th Dragoon Guards

Colonel Richard Sparrow lived at Rookwoods for some twenty years but his sisters, the Misses Sparrow resided there for a much longer period. Col. Sparrow was the youngest son of Basil Sparrow, D.L., J.P., of Gosfield Place who were members of the Sparrow banking family. (The Sparrow Tufnell Bank was taken over by Barclays). Col. Sparrow fought in the Boer War and the First World War being mentioned in Despatches. He was awarded the C.M.G. in 1916 and the D.S.O. in 1918. He had received his commission in 1892 and retired from the army in 1920. He travelled widely and at Rookwoods, housed trophies from rhinoceros to polar bear. A stuffed grizzly bear stood by the entrance door with a tray in its paw to receive visiting cards. He was well known for his valuable collection of animal heads, skins and other trophies shot by him in India, Somaliland, Sierra Leone and Portuguese East Africa. His first wife was Cicely Heyworth (nee Garfitt), the widow of Captain Heyworth of Earls Colne Priory. She was a keen tunny fisher and was the first woman to catch a tunny in the North Sea. Col. and Mrs. Sparrow left Sible Hedingham and moved to Colne Engaine in 1926.

Richard Sparrow photographed in 1909 when he was a Major in the 7th Dragoon Guards.

Sergeant T. Whitehead, D.C.M., M.M., Royal Garrison Artillery

T. Whitehead was the son in law of George Wiffen late of Alexandra Road. This gallant soldier was awarded the Distinguished Conduct Medal on 20th October, 1916 for sticking to the guns under heavy shell fire and keeping up communication by traversing a heavily shelled trench and also repairing three guns under heavy shell fire. He was awarded the Military Medal on 14th October, 1917 for rescuing the wounded and extinguishing the fire during a daylight air raid when an ammunition dump was set on fire. On 31st October, 1917 an ammunition train of 13 trucks was set on fire and Sergeant Whitehead again rescued the wounded and extinguished the fire under heavy shell fire. For this brave action he was awarded a bar to the D.C.M.

Staff-Sergeant William Ross Cowan, M.S.M.

Although William Cowan was not a native of Sible Hedingham, having been born in Madagascar, he moved to the village in 1919 and remained there until his death in 1950. He was a marine engineer by profession and prior to the First World War served in the Merchant Navy travelling to almost every part of the world. In the First World War he joined the Royal Engineers and served in the Mediterranean and Middle East. He became a Staff-Sergeant and was awarded the Meritorious Service Medal. Whilst at Sible Hedingham he set up a haulage business and later ran a tyre vulcanizing business in Swan Street.

The following Sible Hedingham men were mentioned in Despatches during the First World War for distinguished service:–

Company Quarter-Master Sergeant William J. Taylor of the Army Service Corps for distinguished service in the field in 1916.
Sergeant John (Jack) William Coates of the Essex Regiment on the recommendation of General Sir Douglas Haig in 1917. The citation presented to Jack Coates in 1919 was signed by Winston S. Churchill when Secretary of State for War.
Gunner Fred Pannell of the 86th Heavy Battery, Royal Garrison Artillery was mentioned in despatches for Distinguished Service during the defence of Kut-el-Amarah in 1916.

Corporal John William Coates (Jack Coates) (1883–1963) photographed in about 1915. He served in the Essex Regiment and retired with the rank of Acting Sergeant Major. After the war was a founder member of the Hedingham and District Branch of the British Legion. He was employed at Rippers Limited for 50 years and during the Second World War served in the Royal Observer Corps.

Edgar Joseph Spurgeon (Ned Spurgeon) (1883–1973) who served in the Army Service Corps with Motor Transport being a driver in France.

William Willett (1878–1981) in the uniform of the Royal Fusiliers. He also served in the Essex Regiment during the First World War.

Members of the Corder family whilst serving during the First World War.

Fred Corder (1885 – 1961) who served in the Essex Regiment, the Royal Fusiliers, the Machine Gun Corps and the Royal West Kent (Queens Own) Regiment.

His brother, Rifleman John Corder (1876–1922) of the Kings Royal Rifle Corps died from the effects of the war in 1922.

Below are three of their nephews: (1) William Dan Corder (1886 – 1970) who served in the Essex Regiment and later as a Sapper in the Royal Engineers, (2) Herbert Charles Corder (1889 – 1970) of the Royal Army Service Corps and (3) Walter Edward Corder (1896 – 1983) who was also a Rifleman with the Kings Royal Rifle Corps.

Three Sible Hedingham servicemen during the First World War. Seated are Cpl. Ronald Rayner of the Kings Royal Rifles who was wounded and gassed and Percy Corder who also served in the Rifle Brigade and was wounded. Standing in the centre is Stanley Springett who served in the Royal Flying Corps. At the time of writing this book Percy Corder, at the age of 91 years, is the last surviving First World War serviceman in Sible Hedingham out of over 320 men.

Captain Fred Cornish, (1899–1959) was a member of a well known Sible Hedingham brick making family.

In the First World War he served successively in the Essex Yeomanry, the Royal Flying Corps and the 1st East Yorkshire Regiment. He completed over 300 hours flying over enemy lines and downed several of their planes. He was wounded in October, 1917 and being unfit for further flying became a Company Commander in the 1st East Yorkshire Regiment. Between the wars he became County Chairman and a member of the National Executive Council of the British Legion as it then was. In the Second World War he was an Air Raid Precautions Officer and was one time Military Governor of Pachen. In November, 1942 he gave a talk at the request of the B.B.C. on the Fire Guard organisation in England which was relayed to Australia and New Zealand on the Pacific Services short wave.

To commemorate those who gave their lives a war shrine was erected on the wall of the north aisle of the Church and a war memorial in the Churchyard. In addition there is a roll of honour recording those that served on the north wall of the Church.

This handsome war shrine generously given by Mr. & Mrs. Charles T. Halsey of Bridge House was dedicated on 14th April, 1918. It was made from oak removed from H.M.S. Britannia (cadet training ship at Dartmouth 1869–1905) and was furnished with folding doors which when open display the names of the heroes on the interior. The inscription in gold lettering at the head of the shrine is "For God, King and Country". In the middle partition there was a handsome cross made of copper and mounted on oak. A long shelf was provided just below the shrine for floral memorial offerings from the mourning relatives. When originally dedicated 37 names appeared on the shrine but at a later date all 52 names of those fallen were printed on it.

There is also a memorial tablet in the church to Corporal Alan Sidney Elsdon of the East Surrey Regiment who died of wounds received in action on 1st September, 1916 on his 23rd birthday. He was a son of Walter John Elsdon, a builder in the village.

During the early weeks of 1919, Frank Gibson, thoroughly re-decorated the Church Porch and placed an oak seat on either side. He also tiled the floor of the porch and in the centre placed a marble slab bearing the inscription "Sacred to the memory of our fallen heroes, who fell in the Great War, 1914–1918".

The Rector of Sible Hedingham during the First World War was the Rev. Welby Russell Warburton, M.A., photographed here in 1909.

He was born in Sible Hedingham and held the living from 1904 to 1918. He had previously been curate from 1892 and was a Trustee of a number of local charities and became a member of Sible Hedingham Parish Council. He died in September, 1918 and his successor, the Rev. Dr. John Evans was not inducted until March, 1919. During the interregnum many of the services were conducted by the Right Reverend Edmund Nathaniel Powell, D.D., M.A., who was then Vicar of Castle Hedingham. Bishop Powell, a cousin of Lord Baden-Powell, had previously been Lord Bishop of Mashonaland. At the end of the First World War a service of thanksgiving was held in Sible Hedingham Church on 12th November, 1918 which was conducted by Bishop Powell. There was a large congregation and the church bells rung out merry peals under the direction of Lewis Wiseman. Towards the end of November, 1918, the Sible Hedingham poet, Richard Young, had a poem published titled 'PEACE'.

I am pleased the war is over,
There is no fighting now;
The mighty Allied Armies,
Have made the Germans bow.

We will cheer President Wilson,
Foch, Pershing, Haig and Bing;
Their great victory has caused the bells,
Throughout the world to ring.

Pershing and Foch at the German doors did knock,
But, as the doors were rather thin;
They did not stop to open them,
But smashed and entered in.

When they were in, they cast their nets,
And caught an excellent haul;
They caught thousands of Germans in their nets,
With cannons, shells and cannon ball.

We pray that now there will be peace,
Peace that is without fears;
The spears turned into prunninghooks,
And swords turned into ploughshares.

1914-1918.
Sible Hedingham.

Welcome Home.

DINNER AND CONCERT

— TO EX-SERVICE MEN, —

AT THE ASSEMBLY ROOM,

FRIDAY, JANUARY 2nd, 1920.

CHAIRMAN:

REV. DR. EVANS.

: Menu. :

* * *

ROAST BEEF. BOILED BEEF.

ROAST MUTTON.

—

SWEETS.

PLUM PUDDING. MINCE PIES.

FRUIT PIES.

—

CHEESE and CELERY.

—

TOBACCO and CIGARETTES.

BEER and MINERAL WATERS.

: Toast List. :

* * *

"H. M. The King."
THE CHAIRMAN.

* * *

"The Glorious Dead."
REV. G. E. MONSON.

* * *

"H. M. Forces."
E. CORNISH Esq., J.P.

* * *

"Our Guests."
THE CHAIRMAN.

:: Programme. ::

* * *

1. Duet ... "Pensylvaniah,"
   MESSRS. FRANK STEELE & ELLIOTT HOLDEN. ... ...
2. Chorus Song .... "Maryland,"
   MASTER WALLACE BRUCE. ... ...
3. Character Song "The Countryman,"
   MR. W. B. STEELE. ... ...
4. Chorus Song "Fuzzy Wuzzy,"
   MR. FRANK STEELE ... ...
5. Song at Piano "Demobilization,"
   MISS WINNIE STEELE. ... ...
6. Concerted Number "Italians,"
   THF COMPANY. ... ...
7. Chorus Song "The Oopergootic,"
   MR. W. B. STEELE. ... ...
8. Chorus Song "Wire in my lads,"
   MR. ELLIOTT HOLDEN. ... ...
9. Chorus Song "A Bachelor Gay,"
   MR. FRANK STEELE. ... ...
10. Duologue .... "He and She,"
    MISS WINNIE & MR. W. B. STEELE. ... ...

W. H. Root, Caxton Works, Halstead.

SIBLE HEDINGHAM.

WELCOME HOME

Dinner and Concert

To EX-SERVICE MEN,

AT THE

ASSEMBLY ROOM, SIBLE HEDINGHAM,

ON

FRIDAY, 2ND JANUARY, 1920, at 6 p.m.

The Committee request the pleasure of the company of

Mr. Walter Corder

Should you know of any other Demobilized Sailor or Soldier living in Sible Hedingham who has not received a ticket for the dinner please inform Mr. Willis or any Member of the Committee.

After the First World War a Dinner and Concert was given for the ex-service men at the Assembly Rooms which was arranged by the Rev. Evans, Eli Cornish, J.P., Tom Harrington and others. The above is a copy of the menu and an invitation card.

The unveiling and dedication of the war memorial near the south porch of the church on 20th March, 1921. The portland stone cross is of 14th century design to suit the church which is mainly of that period. The memorial has a substantial basement of three steps containing the names of the 52 men who fell during the First World War. (The names of those who fell during the Second World War were later recorded on the memorial.) The unveiling ceremony was performed by Lieut-General Sir Charles James Briggs, K.C.M.G., (1865–1941) of the Kings Dragoon Guards who as a young man had hunted around Sible Hedingham and lived at the Manor House, Wickhambrook. In the centre of the photograph to the right of the cross were the Rector, Dr. John Arthur Evans, D.D., The Rev. (later Canon) Thomas Higham Curling, M.A., of Halstead, Lieut-General Sir Charles Briggs, Colonel Richard Sparrow, Colonel Dewing, Captain William Wright Raynham, D.C.M., (all in uniform), Lieut S.B. Donaldson and Dr. Henry Joseph Twamley.

On the 10th November, 1923 a brass Memorial Tablet was erected in the Mission Room, Swan Street by the Congregational Church. It was unveiled by Sergeant ("Jack") John William Coates, an ex-serviceman of the parish. The tablet also had inscribed upon it the names of the 52 men of Sible Hedingham who gave their lives. The Mission Room was sold by the Congregational Church in 1939 and has for some years been occupied by the Constitutional Club.

There was also a Memorial Tablet which included some Sible Hedingham men at Rippers works and erected on the outside wall of the workshop near the entrance. The oak memorial was made and designed at the works. On the centre panel were engraved the names of the employees who had fallen:–

Bertie Ambrose	Sidney Partridge
Frank Drury	Hubert Ripper
Rupert Hawkins	Edward Thornton
Edward Mead	Alfred Vale

They were surmounted by the words "In Memoriam" and a carved oak cross with a wreath entwined. At the base was the inscription "Their name liveth for evermore 1914–1918". This memorial was unveiled on 10th September, 1921 by James Redgewell, the oldest employee, in the presence of the employees and parents of the fallen, the ceremony being of a private nature.

One Sible Hedingham woman who served during the First World War was Miss Katherine Elizabeth Deeks of Old House and formerly of Sparrows Farm. She was a nurse for some 40 years and being on the Queen Alexandra Nursing Reserve was called up immediately war was declared in 1914 and remained in France nursing prisoners and wounded until 1919. In 1923 she went to China with the China Inland Mission and was stationed at Paoning, high up the Yangtse River until 1927, when with others from the Mission she was sent home when war threatened with Japan.

A few years later, a Miss Margaret Jay who was formerly a teacher at Sible Hedingham School went to China as a teacher to British and American Missionaries children. During the Second World War she was holidaying in Hong Kong when the Japanese took the island and she remained in an Internment Camp until the end of the War.

Committee members representing Castle and Sible Hedingham on the Hedinghams and District Branch of the British Legion in 1925. Back row: ? , Horace Fuller, Albert Smith, Captain Guilding, Jack Coates, Fred Wiseman, James Rand Jackson, Ted Earey, ?
Front row: William Meadowcroft, Arthur Maxim, Fred Williams and Walter Corder

Other committee members representing Sible Hedingham between the wars who are not in the photograph include Captain Fred Cornish, William D. Corder, George L. Foster, Captain William W. Raynham, Harry J.E. Ripper and Thomas M. Vale.

The following is a detailed list of SIBLE HEDINGHAM Servicemen and women who served in the Second World War 1939–1945

(The + indicates those who lost their lives. Their names are also recorded on the war memorial in the churchyard.)

Bernard William Joseph Abraham, Royal Engineers
Dennis Alliston
Bdr. Bert Ambrose, Royal Artillery
Victor S. Ambrose
Craftsman William James Andrews, R.E.M.E.
Eric Robert William Ashby, R.A.F.
Pte. Terry Ashby, Royal Berkshire Regiment
William Harry Bacon, Royal Engineers
Cfn. Douglas Frederick Baggaley, R.E.M.E.
S.Q.M.S. Joseph William Baggaley, R.A.O.C., M.E.F.
Cyril A. Barber
Ronald Barber
L.A.C. Charles William Thomas Bareham, R.A.F.
Eric William Bareham
L.A.C. Robert William Bearham, R.A.F.
W/O Donald Arthur Barker, R.A.F.
Gunner Percy Basil Barker, Royal Artillery
Donald A. Barningham
Alfred Bartlett, Dorset Regiment
Donald Albert Beadle, Royal Navy
Sapper Edward Ernest Beadle, Royal Engineers
Private Walter William Beadle, Norfolk Regiment
J.E. Beaumont
Arthur Bell, Coldstream Guards
Ernest Charles Bell
Corporal John Francis Bell, R.A.F. Service Police
Leslie Gordon Bell
L/Bdr. Christopher Mons Bickers, Royal Artillery
Ronald A. Bonner
Bertie Edward Boreham
Cecil Charles Boreham
Donald F.G. Boreham
Frederick S. Boreham, R.E.M.E.
Herbert Cecil Boreham
H.G. Boreham
Jack Boreham
Corporal Maurice James Boreham, Royal Air Force
S.G. Boreham
Jack Geoffrey Borrett, Royal Air Force
Driver Leonard Bowtle, Royal Engineers Field Company

ACI Gordon Robert Frederick Bradford
Arthur F. Brett, Army
L.A.C. Jack Herbert Brett, R.A.F.
\+ Private Leslie Verdun Brett, Essex Regiment +
Alan Curtis Britton
Maurice S. Bruty
\+ Flight Sergeant Sidney Reginald Bult, Royal Air Force +
Cecil William George Bullock, Pioneer Corps
James William Butcher
Sapper Leonard William Cansell, Royal Engineers
\+ Sergeant Alexander Charles Carter, Royal Air Force +
Alfred Dennis Carter
Dorothy L. Carter, Auxiliary Territorial Service
Petty Officer Fred G. Carter, Royal Navy
Sister Nellie Marie Carter, Queen Alexandra's Imperial Military Nursing Service Reserve
Driver Russell Howard Carter, R.A.S.C. (P.O.W.)
John (Jack) Cartwright, Queen's Royal West Kent Regiment
Sgt. Leslie Nathan Catterwell
Derrick Chaplin
Kenneth G. Chatten
L.A.C.W. Dulcie Jean Clark, W.A.A.F.
Gerald Dennis Clark, Royal Navy
William Samuel George Clarke, Royal Air Force
Brain Clarke
Alan B.D. Cock, Army
Corporal Blance Doreen Cock, W.A.A.F.
Iris E. Cock
Private Norman Sidney Cock, Oxfordshire and Buckinghamshire Light Infantry
Peter Cock, Royal Army Service Corps
L.A.C. Victor Stanley Connell, Royal Air Force
Donald David Copsey
Corporal Beatrice Mary Corder, Auxiliary Territorial Service
Edward Corder
\+ Sergeant Herbert John William Cousins, Home Guard +
John Gerald David Cowlin
Roy A.F. Craven
B.W. Cutts
L.A.C. Harold Douglas Dace, R.A.F.
George W. Daines
A/B Reginald Daines, Royal Navy
A.J. Deal
Arthur Ernest Dixey
D. Dowling
John Dowling, R.A.F.

Philip H. Dowsett
Gunner Douglas Charles Drury, Royal Artillery
Roy Henry Drury
Sapper Samuel Robert Dyson, Royal Engineers
Corporal Donald Robert Earey, Essex Regiment, attached R.A.C.
Pte. Harold John Earey, Essex Regiment
Private Henry Elidor Earey, R.A.S.C., B.L.A.
William Eldridge, R.A.F.
William J. Ennew
Cecil R. Everitt
\+ Frederick E. Everitt +
Herbert John Everitt
H.J. Everitt
John Everitt
Percy William Everitt
Leading Stoker Ronald Reginald Everitt (H.M. Submarine "Sleuth") Royal Navy
Pte. Victor A.W. Everitt
Corporal Gordon Frederick Faiers, Royal Air Force
John H.E. Farrant, Royal Army Pay Corps
Dennis Arthur Faux
\+ Sergeant Thomas Augustus Firman, Home Guard +
Dennis Albert Edward Foster, Royal Navy
Samuel Robson Gardner
Captain Edmund George Geater, R.A.S.C., 6th Airborne Division, M.E.F.
Isabel Betty Gibson
Peggy Elisabeth Maude Gibson
Frederick John Gilbey, Navy
J.P. Gladwell
Leading Cook Alfred L. Gorringe
R.E. Greenway
\+ C. Hale +
Phyllis Margaret Hale, Auxiliary Territorial Service
Seaman Gunner Stephen Harry Hale, Royal Navy
Anthony Frederick Halls, Army
\+ Corporal Cyril Arthur Halls, Home Guard +
Maurice B. Halls
W.P. Halls
D.R. Happe
C.R. Harper
Roy Ernest John Harper
Walter Clarence Harrington, Royal Navy
Sapper D. Charles Richard Harrod, Royal Engineers
Stanley L. Heard, R.A.F.
Barbara J. Hockham
Francis Hockham

Cyril George Holden (Awarded the British Empire Medal in June, 1970)
Sergeant Arnold W. Howard, B.Sc., 52nd (Lowland) Division
Charles M.H. Howe
Phyllis Joyce Nora Hume, Auxiliary Territorial Service
\+ Sergeant Hedley James Iron, Glider Pilot Regiment +
Henry Robert Irvine
Sidney Jarvis
Thomas Jarvis, Royal Marines
Bertie H. Kendall, Royal Navy
George L. Kendall
Roy C. Kendall, R.E.M.E.
A.F. Laver
K.E. Laver
Corporal Samuel Harold Letch, R.A.F.
Driver Stanley W. Letch
Robert G. Mailer
Guardsman Richard Albert Mansfield, Irish Guards
H. Edward Martin
Eric George Mayhew, Royal Marines
E.F. Mathews
Elsie Kate Mead, A.T.S.
Sergeant C. Mead
Stanley George A. Mead
S. Metson
F. Moles
James Moles
Kathleen Florence Moles
Innes Murray
E.G. Needham
Douglas Gordon Newman
Derek M. Newman
James Nicholls
Robert John Nicholls
L. Cpl. Joan Beatrice Noble, Auxiliary Territorial Service
Leading Signalman John Harry Noble
Dennis E.J. Owens
Alfred Herbert Pannell, Royal Navy
W.G. Pannell
S.G. Parsley
Lance Corporal Herbert Pilgrim, B.L.A.
Reginald D. Pilgrim
Stanley D. Pilgrim, Royal Army Service Corps
Roger A. Plaistow
S.A. Plumb
Iris May Proudfoot
Ronald E. Pryke, Royal Navy

+ Petty Officer William Arthur James Pryke, Royal Navy +
Fred Rayner, Royal Navy
H.T.H. Rayner
Percy Rayner, Royal Air Force (Awarded B.E.M. in 1948 for bravery in saving two men from a burning aircraft)
Thomas Redgewell
F.S. Repnan
Flight Lieutenant Harry James Hubert Ripper, Royal Air Force, Bomber Command
Lieutenant Norman Charlton Ripper, Royal Artillery
Charles Henry Rippingale, R.A.F.
Cyril B. Richer
Oliver Rhodes Roberts, Merchant Navy
Lillian D. Robinson
Hector Edward Rose
+ Sapper Reginald E. Rose, Royal Engineers +
A/B, S.T. Spencer Gordon Rose, Royal Navy
Trooper Arthur Richard Ruffle, Tank Corps
Eddie Ruffle
Gordon F. Ruffle
Gladys Emily Ruffle, W.A.A.F.
Gertrude Kate Ruffle, W.A.A.F.
C.E.R.A. John William Ruffle, Royal Navy
Stanley Ruffle, Army
L.A.C. Stephen Frederick Ruffle, R.A.F.
Cfn. William Alfred Ruffle, R.E.M.E.
Gunner Boy Sandford, Royal Artillery Field Regiment
Gunner John V. Scott, Royal Artillery
A.R. Skipp
William R. Slee, Royal Navy
Captain James Blair Sloan
Sapper Frank W. Smith, Royal Engineers
L. Cpl. Frederick William Smith, Royal Artillery
H.S. Smith
Sapper Jack Henry Smith, Royal Engineers
Corporal Kenneth Bertram Smith, Royal Air Force
Pte. Nora Ellen Smith, Auxiliary Territorial Service
P. Smith
P.D. Smith
R. Smith
W/O R.G. Smith, R.A.F.
Walter Frank Smith
L.A.C. Harry Leonard Springett, R.A.F.
A.C. John (Jack) Walter Springett, R.A.F.
Reginald Staines
Albert Richard Stockdale, Army

Sidney R.R. Strudwick
John Joseph Sutton, R.E.M.E.
George Roy Tanner, Royal Air Force
Frederick James Taylor
Horace Taylor
John Leonard Turner
V.J. Turner
Betty Jeanne Vale, Auxiliary Territorial Service/E.F.I.
Flight Lieut. Ernest Alfred Vale, Royal Air Force
C.V. Wade
Samuel D. Waters
\+ Able-Seaman Michael Herbert Ward, Royal Navy +
Bombardier George A. Warner, Maritime Regiment, Royal Artillery
Benjamin Wells
Frederick Wells, R.A.F.
Thomas R. Wells, Army
William A. Wells, R.A.F.
Bert Wheeler, Essex Regiment
Ronald David Wheeler, R.A.F.
Kenneth Walter Wilding, Army
Gunner Roy Frederick Wilding, Royal Artillery
L/A.C. William Ernest Wilding, R.A.F.V.R.
Charles Edward Vincent Williams, 8th Army
Sgt. Ray Williams, Essex Regiment
Frank Ernest Willis, Royal Air Force
J. Winter
Albert Harry Wiseman, Army
Cyril Wiseman
Corporal Herbert William Wiseman, Royal Air Force
Sgt. Maurice W. Wiseman, Essex Regiment
Percy R. Wiseman, Army
Sergeant Eileen May Woodcock, A.T.S.
Corporal Alfred William Worsfold, R.A.F.
Harry Edward Worsfold
Oliver A.C. Wright
David E. Yarham
Pascoe R. Young

The Book of Remembrance in which the above names are contained was provided by public subscription and generous gifts. It is beautifully written on durable hand-made paper and bound in leather. The book is kept in a carved oak case in the church and each Sunday morning a page should be turned so that all those who served are remembered. The book was dedicated at a special service held in the Church in September, 1949 which followed an act of remembrance and thanksgiving at the War Memorial in the Churchyard upon which the names of the fallen were inscribed. In his address, the then Rector, the Rev. George F. Sloan, when referring to the Dedication of the Book stated:

"Those were the names of individuals they all knew,
individuals who had been engaged in that great conflict,
the vastness of which was beyond their knowledge.
They thought of them then, they thought of them now.
Some gave their lives, all gave their peace."

The book was dedicated to the Glory of God and in memory of the men and women of the parish "who gave their peace, that peace might follow pain". Members of the St. Peters Guild of Change Ringers range 720 Changes of Oxford Treble Bob.

Names missing from the original list were:–

Leonard Ambrose, Army
L/Cpl. W. Ambrose, Suffolk Regiment
L.A.C. Edgar Britton, Royal Air Force
Eric Wallace Bult, Royal Air Force
\+ Charles Henry Bourn Dowding, N.A.A.F.I. +
Thomas Robert Marriott Dowling, Merchant Navy
L.A.C. George Hale, Royal Air Force
Sgt. Desmond Thomas Michael Maloney, Queens Royal Lancers, Royal Armoured Corps
L.A.C. Eric R. Rose, R.A.F.V.R.
Sapper William F. Ruffle, B.N.A.F.
Dennis Smith, Royal Air Force
Miriam Ida Smith, N.A.A.F.I.

Sible Hedingham servicemen during the Second World War

Gordon Faiers, Royal Air Force

Three brothers who served in the army: Maurice, Albert and Percy Wiseman.

Douglas Drury, photographed whilst serving in the Home Guard in Sible Hedingham before he joined the Royal Artillery.

In 1942, the Military Medal was awarded to Sergeant Desmond Thomas Michael Maloney, Queens Royal Lancers, Royal Armoured Corps for gallant and distinguished services in the Middle East. Although not a native of Sible Hedingham, his mother lived at Kentish Farm and he visited the village when on leave. He joined the army in 1935, survived the evacuation of Dunkirk and went to the Middle East in 1941.

A former Sible Hedingham resident, Pilot Officer Verdun Ashley Scott, R.A.F.V.R., was awarded the Distinguished Flying Cross in 1942. Although born in Halstead he spent his young life in Sible Hedingham before moving to Sudbury. His father was Alfred Scott, late of Alexandra Road, Sible Hedingham. The award was made for his skill and judgement in bringing home his damaged aircraft after a bombing raid on Bremen in September, 1942. On the return flight, the aircraft of which he was captain, was engaged by an enemy fighter and damaged. The petrol tanks were pierced and the hydraulics were shot away, causing the undercarriage to drop. Despite this he flew home, gradually losing height over the North Sea and carried out a masterly landing in a field. He was killed in action in September, 1943.

Three Sible Hedingham men were mentioned in Desptaches namely Captain Fred Cornish formerly of Tortoise House, L.A.C. Eric R. Rose, R.A.F.V.R., of Grove Cottage and Flight-Lieut. Ernest Alfred Vale then of Christmas Field. Flight-Lieut. Vale took part in 33 bombing sorties over Germany and Italy.

Two very talented blind musicians, Percy and Arthur Bragg, who lived in the village for many years, broadcast on the wireless including the Overseas Service. For these war time broadcasts they gave songs at one piano in the form of a medley of military marches.

During the Second World War, no less than seven allied aircraft crashed in Sible Hedingham including two R.A.F. in 1941 and 1942 and five U.S.A.A.F. all in 1944.

The above photograph shows the remains of a U.S.A.A.F., B17 Flying Fortress (No.42–31278) from the nearby Ridgewell Airfield (381st Bomb Group of the Eighth Air Force) which had crashed on take off at Blooms Farm, the exact location being 120 yards north of Redbeards Wood.

The crash occurred on the 4th January, 1944 at 07.50 hours when all ten members of the crew were killed, the aircraft being fully loaded for a mission.

Later in 1944, four U.S.A.A.F. Havocs crashed in Sible Hedingham; one from Wethersfield Airfield on 14th February near Barnards Farm and on 13th August two more from Wethersfield crashed at Cuckoo Farm. Finally on 25th August, 1944 a Havoc from Gosfield Airfield crashed at Southey Green.

In addition there were at least ten bombings and similar incidents suffered by the village between September, 1940 and December, 1944. In September and October, 1940 there were no less than five bombings including a land mine at Cut Maple, a high explosive bomb at Braintree Corner and six high explosive bombs in a field near Rippers works and the Railway Station. The bomb which fell at Braintree Corner on 23rd September, 1940 caused extensive damage over a wide area of the village including the Primary School. Many others also caused damage, but it is understood that only one life was lost, being that of a woman who died of shock. This occurred on 29th September, 1944 when a flying bomb fell near Hostages Farm causing damage to 21 houses and the Primary School. Another flying bomb which fell on 13th December, 1944 damaged Rookwoods, the Secondary School, Rippers works and the Gas Office.

Some members of the Sible Hedingham Home Guard (No.1 Platoon, D. Company, 15th Battalion of the Essex Home Guard) in front of their headquarters, Hedingham Secondary Modern School as it then was. The white arm bands denote stretcher bearers. In the back row, left to right are: Joe Moules, Herbert Everitt and Samuel Earey. On the left of the second row is Ernest Finch and on the extreme right is Eddie Letch. Standing in front are the platoon commander, Lt. Norman Vagg and Medical Officer, Captain Philip Putnam. Norman Vagg was Verger of Sible Hedingham Church for nearly 60 years and Philip Putnam was a Doctor of Medicine practising in Sible Hedingham and Great Yeldham for some 40 years.

The High Street Green section of the A.R.P. at Sible Hedingham. Left to right, back row: Maurice Everitt, John Smith, Cecil Smith, Fred Wiseman, ? ? , Robert Hornsby. Front row: Horace Hale, Cecil Goodchild, Aubrey Letch, Charles Warren, Charles Britton.

Sible and Castle Hedingham men who served in the Royal Observer Corps during the Second World War photographed at Sudbury Hill, Castle Hedingham in about 1939. Left to right, back row: Bill Lane, Ted Marjoram, Boyd Davey, Thomas Vale, Bob Howe, Rodney Hatfield. Second row: Cyril Baines, M.M., Harold Baines, William F. Meadowcroft, Bertram Hogarth, Albert Smith, Sidney Blake, John (Jack) Coates. Front row: Stanley Finch, Bill Clark, John Guilding, Tills Smith, Ernie Hurry, Les Pryke. The Observers were also Special Constables and some are wearing their Special Constable arm bands on their left arms.

Sible Hedingham residents and children celebrating V.E. Day, 8th May, 1945, in the yard behind the White Lion Public House in Church Street. The cottages which stood at the back of the Lion yard were later demolished.

The village school closed for three days to celebrate the cessation of hostilities in Europe and a large bonfire was lit on the Recreation Ground. On 22nd June, 1946 a peal was rung on St. Peters Church bells in honour of Victory Day (and an engagement). The Essex Association of Change Ringers rang a peal of Kent Treble Bob Major, 5,088 changes in 3 hours 8 minutes. The ringers were Ernest Brown (treble), Reginald Rippingale (2), Olave E. Broyd (3), Cecil J. Barker (4), Simon Dace (5), Thomas Bird (6), Robert Young (7), and Ernest W. Pye (Tenor).

THE SIBLE HEDINGHAM BRASS BAND AND DANCE BANDS

In 1922 the Sible Hedingham Brass Band was formed. This photograph shows the late Percy Ralph Bareham in the band uniform.

Frederick Hunt, A. Eyres and Lewis Wiseman were successively bandmasters and other members included Joseph Baggaley, Cecil Chatten, Ernest Chatten, Eddie Cocks, Bert Corder, Edward Corder, William James Drury, Bertie Everitt, Horace Fuller, Robert Howe, Willie Kendall, William Lodge, Frank Mead, Tom Parsons, Charles Powell and Arthur Wash. Frederick Hunt of Halstead had been one of the original members of Halstead Town Band when it was formed in 1894. He became one of the founders of the Hedingham Brass Band and acted as Bandmaster for its first season. Lewis Wiseman also took a leading part in the formation of the band of which he was Hon. Secretary and Treasurer. His life long interest was in bell ringing, being a master ringer of the Essex Association of Bell Ringers and leader of the ringers at Sible Hedingham Church. Following a serious fire on 1st May, 1938 at a hall in Swan Street, where the band practised, they lost all their instruments including a large drum, side drum, cymbals, music stands, music and other items. This necessitated the suspension of all practice and playing for the season. With the outbreak of war the following year the band was sadly wound up when several members joined H.M. Forces. After the War, the band restarted in October, 1948 with Bertie Everitt as Conductor. The following year it was taken over by the Hedingham and District Branch of the British Legion.

'The Syncopated Six Dance Band' photographed in the former Assembly Rooms, Swan Street in 1937. Left to Right: Leonard Mitson, Jack Palmer, Mrs. Chambers, P.C. Chambers, Basil Ruffle, Bob Bearham (leader of the band) and Billy Carter. The Band Secretary was Miss Lily Harrington who took an active part in arranging Dances at the Assembly Rooms for charitable causes.

There was another Dance Band in the village which had been formed by Lewis Wiseman who was leader and violinist. Other members of this Jazz Band included Jack Wiseman, William Lodge, Cyril Baines and Miss Constance Cook.

THE PLAZA CINEMA

The former Plaza Cinema, Swan Street photographed in August, 1929.

It was built between March and August that year by E.G. French, a Birdbrook builder. The opening took place on 29th August, 1929 and the first film was Harold Lloyd in "Speedy". The seating capacity was 294. The proprietors were Greenfells Limited of which Sidney Reach of Southey Green was manager until George Jonah Howell of Bakers Farm became owner. The cinema closed in 1959 and after standing empty for some years the building was altered and became the Akabar Club for a short time in about 1970 and was later converted to its present use as Citroen Car showrooms.

-: PLAZA :-

SIBLE HEDINGHAM.

This Hall will be Opened on THURSDAY, AUGUST 29th,

with HAROLD LLOYD in—

"SPEEDY,"

ALSO

"Love's Springtime,"

A Beautiful Picture, and

"BELPHEGOR,"

The Greatest Mystery Serial ever made.

It's Lavish. It's Weird. It's Haunting. It's Haunted.

Pathe Super Gazette.

Next Mon., Tues, Wed.—Clive Brook in "Forgotten Faces."

TIMES—Mon. till Fri., 7.30, Sat. Matinee, 2.30. Evening 6.0 and 8.15,

Prices of Admission: 1/6, 1/-, 9d. and 6d,

Children Half-price to 1/6 and 1/-, Matinee 8d., 4d. and 6d.

An advertisement for the opening of the Plaza Cinema from the Halstead Gazette of 23rd August, 1929.

FOOTBALL, BOWLS, CRICKET AND TENNIS

The Sible Hedingham Favourites Football team of 1921. Left to right, back row: Ernie Boreham, Norman Vagg, Alec Hale, Alfred Ambrose and B. Hall. Centre row: Horace Hale, Lionel Harper and William Mansfield. Front row: Fred Boreham, Tom Wheeler, Kimberley Harper, Stanley Wilding and Fred Everitt.

Hedingham Baptist Church Football Club. Left to right, back row: Walter Springett, Harry Springett, Billy Morton, Thomas Wells, Edward Corder, Bert Ambrose, George King, Ernie Boreham. Front row: Stanley Mead, ? ? , Telford Morton, Leslie Catterwell.

Sible Hedingham Cricketers photographed at Finches Farm including Eli Cornish, Tom Harrington, Walter Harrington and William Mower.

Sible Hedingham Cricketers photographed at Finches Farm about 1912 or 1913. Back row: John Drury, Charlie Downs (of Gestingthorpe), Levi Letch, Tom Harrington, Eli Cornish, ? Bonner. Centre row: George Rouse (Hostage Farm), Horace Hale, William Watson (Red House Farm), ? Watson, junior, Bill Redgewell, Sydney Hale, Scott Hale, Charlie Bonner, Bill Ashby, Charlie Wheeler. Front row: Phil Warren, Aubrey Letch, George Elsdon, George Letch, unknown, Arthur Thomas Mortimer and "Corse" Wilson.

For many years the Bell Inn had a Bowls Team and their 'Green' was located at the rear of the Alms Houses the chimneys of which can be seen in the background. The players in about 1930 were, left to right: Jim Andrews, Bob Brett, Frederick Jacques, Tom Harrington (the Bell), Mark Newman (Butcher), Arthur Thomas Mortimer (Draper of Castle Hedingham), Robert Howe (Plumber of Castle Hedingham) and George Sylvester (Landlord of the Crown Public House at Castle Hedingham). Other players in the Bell Bowls Team included: Fred Corder, William Lodge, Bert Basham, Bill Bareham, Walter Britton.

Tennis Court at Tortoise House, Wethersfield Road c. 1920's with Captain Fred Cornish and his father Eli Cornish, J.P., in the foreground and Jessie Metson and her husband Charles Metson in the backgfound. Jessie Metson was a daughter of Eli Cornish. The tennis court was originally the site of the first clay pit for the adjacent Tortoise brickworks owned by Eli Cornish. Tortoise House was built by him in 1889 with red bricks made at his brickworks.

SIBLE HEDINGHAM SCOUTS

The Sible Hedingham troop of Boy Scouts was one of the first to be started in Essex. The inaugural meeting was held on the lawn of Tortoise House by invitation of Eli Cornish, J.P., in August, 1910. This photograph was taken on 7th August, 1911 at Hilton House with Scout Masters William Raynham and Jack Coates. The boys are:–

V. Sandford, B. Rayner, A. Carter, E. Brown, G. Staines, P. Pilgrim, F. King, F. Cox, R. Rayner, J. Pilgrim, B. Howe, B. King, C. Smith, B. Cutler, S. Dury, R. Vale and Alfred Vale. The two Scout Masters and some of the boys later served in the First World War.

The Sible Hedingham troop of Boy Scouts photographed at their Camp on the Park at Gosfield Hall Estate in 1914.

ONE FINAL SCENE

Finally, of all the photographs reproduced in this book, showing areas of Sible Hedingham which have changed considerably over the years, perhaps no view has altered so noticeably as this one of Brook Meadow. The only landmark was the Sugar Loaves Public House on the right which still survives. The Brook Meadow Housing Estate was later built for the former Halstead Rural District Council in 1947/48. The estate consisted of 58 houses for which the architect was Douglas G. Armstrong of Braintree. To the left, the County Library (formerly the site of the Fire Station), a car showrooms (previously the Plaza Cinema) and a shop now stand. Sadly, the rural scene pictured above has gone forever. The quiet country lane, free from traffic, is now the main A604 and even the large trees have been felled. It is hoped that this final photograph will serve as a reminder that Sible Hedingham is continually changing and of the importance to record all scenes and aspects of village life before they disappear forever.

BIBLIOGRAPHY

A Guide to the Church of St. Peter, Sible Hedingham	Canon G. Howard-Davies	
Castle Hedingham: Its History and Associations	Henry Ranger	1887
East Essex and Halstead Times		
Essex	Arthur Mee	1942
Essex Countryside Magazines		
Essex in the Twentieth Century	Contemporary Biographies	1909
Essex Reviews		
Essex River Colne its tributaries and creeks	Vernon Clarke	1979
Essex Windmills, Millers and Millwrights (Vol.IV)	Kenneth G. Farries	1985
Essex at Work (1700–1815)	A.F.J. Brown	1969
Halstead and Colne Valley at War (1939–1945)	Dave Osborne	1983
Halstead Gazettes		
Kelly's, White's and Post Office Directories of Essex		
Memoirs of Sir John Hawkwood (and additions)		1782 1784
Micah Corder and his Descendants	Francis Corder Clayton	1885
Monuments of North-West Essex		1916
Recollections of an old Woodpecker	H. Tucker Ripper	1948
Ripper Woodwork	Rippers Limited	1929
Schools and Scholars in Halstead and District	Mary Downey and Doreen Potts	1986
Secret Essex	Glyn Morgan	1982
Sible Hedingham Church Registers		
Sible Hedingham Parish Magazines		
Sir John Hawkwood	John Temple-Leader and Giuseppe Marcotti	1889
Some Essex Watermills (Second edition)	Hervey Benham	1983
The Hedinghams through Three Centuries 1700–1975	Hedingham W.E.A.	
The Industrial Archaeology of East Anglia	David Alderton and John Booker	1980
The Place-names of Essex	P.H. Reaney	1969
The Trade Signs of Essex	Miller Christy	1887
Vintage Steam Owners and Operators of the Colne Valley Area	Robin A. Harding	1985